COMFORT ZONE
INVESTING

Also by Ted Allrich

The On-Line Investor

COMFORT ZONE
INVESTING

Build Wealth and
Sleep Well at Night

TED ALLRICH

St. Martin's Press ⚹ New York

www.stmartins.com

Library of Congress Cataloging-in-Publication Data

Allrich, Ted.
    Comfort zone investing : build wealth and sleep well at night / Ted Allrich.
        p. cm.
    ISBN-13: 978-0-312-35894-5
    ISBN-10: 0-312-35894-6
    1. Investments—Handbooks, manuals, etc. I. Title.

HG4527.A45 2007
332.6—dc22

                                                                        2006049776

First Edition: February 2007

10 9 8 7 6 5 4 3 2 1

To my lovely and wonderful daughter, Alison,
and to Darci, the most beautiful, intelligent, and
kind goddess who could have chosen anyone
and picked me. I will be forever grateful.

Contents

Acknowledgments

First to George Witte for another great title and for his graciousness. Thanks to Michael Larsen for his enthusiasm for the book since the proposal. To Ethan Friedman for his initial help. To Phil Revzin for redefining fast turnaround.

Introduction

The best time to invest is when you have money.

—*Sir John Templeton, founder, Templeton Funds*

Doesn't help much, does it?

You probably already knew that. But where to invest, what to invest in, and how to invest are the questions that most often need answering. Those decisions determine if you keep your money and/or make it grow. This book is about the where, what, and how of investing. It will guide you to investments that will make you comfortable, that put you in your personal Comfort Zone.

If you're starting to invest, or have money in the stock market but don't have the greatest confidence, keep reading. If you are scared by investing, definitely keep reading. I'll get you to your Comfort Zone so you can invest with a calmness most people don't have.

You'll find information that's easy to understand, described in simple language that explains the most important aspects of the stock market and how to make better choices for investing. You'll read about decisions investors make that push them out of their Comfort Zones, learn how to recognize what news will most likely move the market, discover secrets of investing pros, and learn how to make money without fear and stress.

As I wrote this book, I thought of my two children, each in their twenties. I also imagined retiring nurses, plumbers, teachers, interior designers, and scientists, recently divorced men and women, the newly widowed, and sons and daughters with recent inheritances. This book is for all of them and many more, who are struggling with investments that only add to their already stressful lives. There are many investment choices available for every person's Comfort Zone. Up until now, though, the information on all these choices has been hard to find, too scattered, or nonexistent.

Most investors don't take the time or haven't found enough answers in other sources to fully know what they're doing. I guarantee once you've read this book and use the material in it, you'll have a new perspective on investing and reach a Comfort Zone you didn't know existed. These are things I wish I had known thirty years ago when I started investing and launched a career on Wall Street.

I can't guarantee every stock you buy will be a winner. In fact, I know you'll have some losers. We all do. They're part of investing. But by understanding what makes a great stock, what influences the stock market, and how to build a portfolio, you will create your own Comfort Zone and achieve a peace of mind most investors never reach.

Investing is a journey. I've tried to make this part fun. Come along with me and I'll show what you need to know, what's important for success. Once you've read this book and understand it, you'll find a new investing level: your own Comfort Zone.

PART ONE

INVEST WITHOUT STRESS

1

Using Mutual Funds

Money is better than poverty, if only for financial reasons.

—*Woody Allen*

Money. It's what we all want, and need—for so many different reasons. Once we've got the basic necessities covered, we have to provide for the future, for ourselves and our children. In order to do that, we have many investment choices. Too many. Some are very risky. Some aren't. Some work better for older investors, some for younger ones.

That's what makes investors nervous. They don't know which investments are right for them. Or they don't know about all the choices. Or they don't understand how investing really works.

This book will change all that. After you've read it, you'll have more knowledge about investing than anyone but the investment pros. Later in the book, I'll even share some of their intelligence so you can use it. You'll reach a new level of understanding about stocks, mutual funds, and bonds. You'll also understand what makes markets move. You'll be much more educated about the ways of the investing world and how to exploit its many facets. You'll choose the right investments for your goals. You'll enter into your own Comfort Zone.

A good way to start is by hiring a professional, someone who will manage your money while you learn more about investing. You think you don't have enough money for a pro? You're wrong. You can do it by using mutual funds.

Mutual funds are the luxury limos for cruising to your Comfort Zone. They offer professional management and diversification. They can help fill a portfolio with specialized investments that are well beyond the average investor's understanding. I'm a big fan of mutual funds and encourage you to start your investing with them.

In this chapter, you'll see reference to a Core Portfolio. Chapter 6 is dedicated to building this important component of Comfort Zone investing.

Types of Mutual Funds

There are open-end funds, closed-end funds, and exchange-traded funds. Each has unique attributes, but they all have certain commonalities:

1. **A fund offers certain types of investments, articulated in its prospectus.** You should always read the prospectus of any fund in which you have an interest before you invest in it. The prospectus tells you everything about the fund, such as the fees it charges, the investments it makes, the tenure of the management, etc. These are all important things to know before you send in your money. Most prospectuses are summarized online at the fund's Web site and/or on a Web site like Morningstar (www.morningstar.com). Every fund will send a prospectus upon request.

2. **All funds work like this:** They gather money from many individuals, pool it together, and then buy stocks and/or bonds in specific ways that are described in the fund's prospectus. In other words, you are putting your money in with that of many other investors to take advantage of the expertise of the fund's managers, as well as the efficiencies that larger holdings of equities or bonds will give.

3. **There are funds for almost every investment imaginable.** Funds range from investing in large stocks to buying gold to investing in

foreign bonds to buying U.S. Treasuries. There is no end to the selection of funds. That's why they're the best way to get started in general or within an industry. You can buy the fund while you continue learning, and eventually choose and buy specific stocks when you feel you know enough.

4. **Mutual funds can be bought directly from the funds themselves, either through a Web site, or by mailing in the money, or delivering it in person, or through brokers.** Funds that are traded on exchanges (exchange-traded funds or closed-end funds—both explained later) are bought through a broker because they trade like stocks.

5. **Fees.** There are a number of possible fees that must be disclosed in the prospectus of a fund. Here is a list of the most common ones. It's rare that a fund will charge all of these fees but sometimes they do. You don't want to own those. The fewer the fees, the more of your money goes to work for you.

   • **Up-front fee or commission or load.** This is charged when you buy the fund. If it's 5%, that means for every $1 you put in, only 95 cents finds its way into the fund. Part of that nickel goes to the people who run the fund and part of it goes to the brokers who sell it.

   • **Marketing fees (also known as 12b-1 fees).** This is a charge many funds have that helps them pay for selling the fund to new investors. The maximum charge allowable is .75% of assets. This is deducted every year from the fund's total assets, before you would get any of your money back. There are funds that do not charge any marketing fees.

   • **Management fees.** This is how the managers of the fund get paid for managing your money. This is one fee you can't and shouldn't avoid. Would you work for free?

   • **Back-end fees and level loads.** Some funds will charge you for leaving. Called a "back-end fee," this fee is rare, but it is sometimes there. Don't buy a fund with one of these attached. I can guarantee you there is another fund with performance just as good and no back-end fee. These fees usually decrease over time and almost always are waived after 10 years. Another rare fee is the "level load," which requires that you pay a certain amount of your return every year. Again, not seen very often, but if it's in there, you don't want it.

6. **Share classes.** Some funds offer three different ways to buy the fund. They use shares designated as "A", "B," or "C" class shares. The A-class shares usually have a front-end load. The B shares usually have a back-end load. The C shares have no load but are charged a higher set of annual charges such as the marketing and administration fees. Again, there are plenty of funds that don't charge any fees for buying or selling them or the fee is so low that it's not going to noticeably change your wealth. Actively seek these out.

7. **Price volatility.** Every fund will go up and down in price. That's because stocks and bonds go up and down in price. The more general the fund, such as Growth and Income, the more the fund will move with the general market. If you own an index fund, it will follow exactly what the index does, the Standard & Poor's 500 Index, for example. The general funds will have less price volatility than specialized funds, such as gold or biotech or technology. With these funds you don't get diversification among industries. That's the very reason you own one. You have a fund that buys many different stocks within one industry. If that industry is having a rough time, suffering from an industry-specific problem, then the fund invested only in that industry is going to have very poor performance. It's going to suffer and so will you. That's why industry-specific funds can't hold more than 5% of your portfolio if you're going to stay in the Comfort Zone. Just having a fund doesn't get you away from the volatility of a specific industry. General funds, on the other hand, can give you plenty of diversity and can easily occupy 10% of your portfolio and more if you're going to start with them.

Open-End Mutual Funds

The most common mutual fund is known as an open-end fund. The description refers to the fact that it is open to new investors and will take in their money to add to the pool already created by other investors. (When an open-end fund reaches its maximum size, it will be "closed" to outside investors, but this is different from the way a "closed-end fund" works, which I'll explain next. Very few open-end funds are closed to new investors.)

The open-end fund sells shares based on the price at the close of business. It does not trade on an exchange or over the counter. It sells to or buys back its shares from investors directly, though you can place your order through a stock broker or can buy or sell directly with the fund. The price of the fund's shares is based on the Net Asset Value (NAV), which is determined by adding up the value of the shares and cash in the fund and dividing by the number of shares outstanding. That calculation is done at the close of every business day.

When you want to buy or sell an open-end mutual fund, you pay the NAV, plus or minus a broker's commission, if applicable. Remember, many funds are "no load" funds, meaning there is no up-front charge to buy or when you sell. Some funds even have that arrangement with a broker so all of your money is put to work when you buy it.

When you put in your order, you buy it the next day. Your share price is based on the closing price of the day on which you placed your order. In other words, if you buy an open-end fund on Monday, you won't actually buy it until Tuesday, based on the NAV price of Monday's close.

Open-end funds come in every variety you want. There are index funds, biotech funds, large-cap funds (focusing on large stocks), small-cap funds (smaller companies), mid-cap funds, growth and income funds, etc. You can get a good read on all the types of funds by looking at a mutual fund screening program found on Yahoo!Finance or AOL or MarketWatch or Morningstar. (See Web Sites on page 212 for the links).

The screening programs list all the funds in a category with links to a full description of each of them. A good exercise would be to go to Yahoo!Finance now and look at the Mutual Fund resources found under the Mutual Funds headline on the left of the page, then click on Screener.

So of all the funds there, which should you buy? Go to the Core Portfolio (chapter 6) for your first one or two choices. On page 11, I describe what to look for in funds. If you want to go beyond the Core Portfolio individual stock needs, and substitute an energy fund for the oil stock that is recommended in the core holdings, that's a good way to start. After you feel comfortable in stock investing, you can sell that fund and buy the individual oil stocks.

You can use funds for almost any of the core holdings, because a mutual fund does a great job of helping an investor get into sectors needed for diversification but may not have the expertise for the individual stocks they want to own. That's why funds were originally developed: to help the small investor in the stock market.

The Closed-End Fund

This fund is not "closed" to investors. Rather it is closed at the day it is funded and then trades its shares on an exchange so you can buy and sell the fund like a stock. (A great Web site that goes into many details about closed-end funds (CEF) is www.closed-endfunds.com. Another one is at the Securities and Exchange Commission site: www.sec.gov/answers/mfclose.htm.)

The main differences between the closed-end and open-end funds is the way they are priced and traded. I've described the calculation for the NAV for open-end funds. The same calculation is used for the NAV for closed-end funds. They trade all day at a premium or a discount to the NAV with their own ticker symbol, on an exchange. It makes them very easy to buy or sell.

When a closed-end fund begins its life, it raises money by describing a certain expertise it will provide for investors. It may propose investing in Japanese stocks. If enough investors subscribe to that idea, they give their money to the fund, and the fund closes, working only with the money raised on the initial offering. In other words, the amount of money the fund gets when it starts is all it will have to invest. It is not open-ended. The fund is assigned a ticker symbol and then starts to trade on an exchange.

The fund will have a bid and an ask, just like a stock. And here is where closed-end funds get interesting. Sometimes, they trade at a discount to their NAV. Sometimes they trade at a premium. So smart investors can buy $1 worth of the fund for 90 cents or less at times. Or they can sell $1 worth of the fund at $1.10 or higher at times. In other words, these funds don't trade at their NAVs but instead at a price set by the market, which is sometimes above or below or right at the NAV. How is this possible?

It has to do with perceptions of things to come. When investors feel things will continue to get worse, they sell their stocks, even though the price is too far below the real value for the stocks. The same is true for closed-end funds. If investors think the industries or countries that the fund specializes in will be doing poorly in the future, they will sell those funds, no matter the true value of the fund. Sometimes the panic gets so bad that sales are made at 15% to 20% of a discount to the NAV. Other times, when an area is extremely hot, as were Internet funds in the late '90s, investors get stupid and pay 15% to 20% more than the value of the fund, just so they can get into it. Those hot funds have a way of cooling way off, and cold funds have a way of moving toward their NAV, and below, after reality hits investors.

If you think about it, a closed-end fund can always liquidate itself. When it does, the investor would receive the NAV for their shares. So if you buy it for a discount, you have a decent chance of making money, no matter what the fund does. Of course, a discount can always go to a deeper discount. But if you study specific funds and see what their ranges for discounts and premiums have been, you can buy and sell these funds at the right times.

Good sources for finding CEFs are the Value Line Investor Survey (www.valueline.com), which is also available in print at your local library or by subscription; Morningstar (www.morningstar.com), also available in print at your local library or by subscription; a general site: www.closed -endfunds.com (note this is a different Web site from one with a very similar URL mentioned earlier in the chapter, www.closed-endfunds.com); and one more: www.site-by-site.com/usa/cef/cef.htm. By looking at these sites, and reading their general articles, then investigating individual

CEFs, you'll get comfortable with this type of fund. They can be incredible bargains and are easily bought and sold. They are well worth your effort.

Exchange-Traded Funds (ETFs)

An ETF is a specialized closed-end fund introduced on the American Stock Exchange in 1993. As of this writing there are more than $200 billion worth of ETFs and 140 different ones being traded. What's the distinction between a closed-end fund and an ETF? Very little. But each ETF is created to track an index such as a broad stock or bond market index such as the NASDAQ-100, a stock industry sector, or an international stock market.

An ETF trades like a stock, just like a CEF does. You can buy or sell it during the trading day, without waiting for the end of the day to determine the NAV. The NAV for an ETF is always available so you know the discount or premium when you buy or sell it. You pay straight brokerage commissions on each trade. There is no "load" or upfront fees to buy these funds. So if you have a discount brokerage account, you can buy or sell them for a small commission. They also tend to have lower capital gains taxes attached to them because the funds hold their securities longer. For example, if you buy an ETF that tracks the NASDAQ-100, there is no need for the fund to buy or sell the stocks in the index once they have a position in them. When new securities are added or deleted, the fund has to accommodate them, but other than that, the fund doesn't need to make trades.

That also keeps the expenses down for the ETFs. They're not "actively" managed as other funds are. Since they track an index, they don't require managers to constantly look to sell overvalued shares or buy undervalued ones. There are also index mutual funds that are not actively managed and have lower expenses.

For more information on ETFs, please see these sites. The American Stock Exchange (www.amex.com) and NASDAQ (www.nasdaq.com) both have screens that describe and list ETFs on their sites.

ETFs are great for filling the Core Portfolio need for buying an index fund or for a broad investment in the technology industry or other specialty area. You can find a listing of ETFs at the sites above, as well as on Yahoo!Finance (http://finance.yahoo.com/etf); MarketWatch (www.market watch.com); or AOL (keyword ETF Center).

What to Look for in Funds

What you're looking for in a good mutual fund is strong performance over ten years. Some growth funds, especially those that specialize in smaller companies, do very well during a bull market, then give it all back when the market turns sour. In a ten-year period, a fund will experience both good and bad markets. The funds that do well in both, and by that I mean they don't lose as much as their competition in bad markets, are the ones you want.

The Morningstar system ranks funds with a star system, with five stars as the highest. Just because a fund has five stars does not mean it's safe. It does mean management has produced good results given the criteria of the fund through good and bad times. Look for five-star funds but know they will still have volatility.

The Micro-Cap ETF

A type of mutual fund for investing in new companies is called a micro-cap ETF. The micro-cap means extremely small companies, usually having a market cap of $50 million to $500 million. *Market cap* is short for market capitalization, or the *market value* of a company, which is calculated by multiplying the number of shares times the market price of a stock. Micro-cap stocks are very small companies, and most of them are new to the public market.

A good example of a micro-cap fund is the Barclays Global Investors Fund, which tracks U.S. micro-cap stocks. It has the unusual name of iShares Russell Microcap Index Fund. The ticker symbol is IWC. The fund trades on the New York Stock Exchange, and it tracks the bottom 3% of the U.S. stock market by market capitalization. In other words, most of the smallest stocks that are publicly traded are included. It holds the smallest 1,000 securities in the small-cap Russell 2000 index as well as the next 1,000 stocks below the index, the ones that are too small to be in the Russell 2000. There are no stocks below $1 or stocks that trade only in the "pink sheets," which are stocks that don't qualify for listing on the exchanges or the National Association of Securities Dealers Automated Quotes (NASDAQ). These criteria keep out many marginal stocks.

There are several other micro-cap funds. Two more are managed by PowerShares Exchange Trust Fund, also known as Zacks Micro Cap Portfolio, which trades on the American Exchange with the symbol of PZI; another is managed by First Trust Advisors (FTACX), traded on Nasdaq. These funds will give you a chance to participate in new companies through another avenue: the exchange-traded fund.

Too Much Enthusiasm

This is a good time to mention enthusiasm and investing. Usually too much enthusiasm is bad for your wealth. It blurs your reasoning and makes you do things quickly that you can regret for a long time. For example, you may read about an aggressive mutual fund that just reported a year where it made more than 100% on its money. That happens in bull markets. But maybe that fund used leverage—in other words, it borrowed to buy more stock—and had spectacular luck. Or maybe the market was kind and took every stock higher that year. When the market turns south, however, that method of investing is deadly.

And often, that's what happens. A mutual fund that reports a great year usually doesn't have two of them in a row, because most of the time an investment style doesn't last very long. As mentioned before, you're looking for a fund that has shown good performance over several years, preferably ten or more. Don't buy a fund based on one year's numbers. It's almost guaranteed to give some or most of that back in the next. Don't let your initial euphoria blind you into quickly buying anything. Go after the tried and true, not the hottest fund from last year.

International Mutual Funds

There are many types of international mutual funds. Some of them invest in a region such as Asia/Pacific. Others invest only in one country, while some fund managers roam the globe looking for great stocks no matter where they're headquartered.

There are some caveats that go with international investing you should keep in mind. There is the usual risk involved in any stock investment, only a little more. That's because no other country has the advanced capital markets we take for granted here in the United States. We have the Securities and Exchange Commission (SEC) to make sure companies fully disclose all their activities. We have the National Association of Securities Dealers (NASD) to monitor stockbrokers and dealers, to make sure they are dealing honestly with the public.

In other economically developed countries there are decent capital markets with safeguards in place but nothing like those in the United States. The less developed countries have less developed capital markets. If you're buying a fund that specializes in a new market, expect some nasty surprises once in a while.

But that's where the advantages of a mutual fund come in: you have wide diversification because the fund will buy many stocks in the country, and you'll have professional management. The pros know the dangers that lie beneath the balance sheets.

One of my friends was a manager for a large international fund specializing in South America. He said the way he started to find companies to invest in was to ask his contacts in a country which businesses were honest. That one criterion helped him avoid many, but not all, problems.

If you're going to try to pick individual stocks in foreign countries trading on foreign exchanges, you'll find it very difficult to get timely information. Many of the companies are only required to report once a year. By the time you receive an annual report it will be history you're reading, not current business.

Another concern is currency risk. Your returns will be helped or hurt by what the dollar does. Investing in foreign stocks means you have to buy them in foreign currencies. If the dollar strengthens against the currency, you can lose some or all of your profits when you sell the stock and turn those proceeds into dollars. If you have a loss from the investment, the currency hit only pours salt in the wound. One-country mutual funds carry extreme currency risk.

Where to Find International Funds

There are many good screening programs on the Web that can help you find international or country-specific mutual funds.

To find a fund, click on one option in each box. Following is an example for finding a good international fund using Yahoo!Finance: http://screen .yahoo.com/funds.html.

Category: Any International Stock Fund

Fund Family: Any

Rank in Category: Top 30%. (You don't want only the best 10%. Remember what's hot last year, most likely isn't this year.)

Manager Tenure: Longer than 10 years. You want someone with plenty of experience at the helm.

Ratings: Minimum 4 stars, maximum 5 stars. (This is on the Morningstar scale where 5 is the best.)

Return Rating: "Minimum Average," "Maximum Above Average." (Again, Morningstar ratings and you don't want the "High" return because that's where the most risk is.)

Risk Rating: "Minimum Below Average," "Maximum Average." (We're looking for the Comfort Zone, not the highest risk.)

Performance Returns: YTD (means Year to Date) Up more than 0%
1-Year Return: Up More Than 5%.
3-Year Return Annualized: More Than 10%
5-Year Return Annualized: More Than 15%

Minimum Initial Investment: Less than $250. This category will screen funds that take the amount of money you wish to invest. Some funds have very high minimums and are for institutions. Put in the amount of money you want to invest internationally. I would recommend no more than 10% of your available investment money.

Front Load: "No Load." Always choose "No Load" first. If you can't find a fund with "No Load" (which means no up-front commission fees), then choose the one with the lowest fee. There is no long-term correlation between up-front fees and performance.

Total Expense: Less than 1.5%. In international funds, fees are higher because costs are more. Managers need to travel often and to go longer distances.

Holdings: *Net Assets:* Minimum of $250 million, maximum of $1 billion. Funds that have too much money sometimes chase after stocks that are marginal. If a fund has too little, it can't create a good diversified portfolio.

Turnover: Minimum of 10%, maximum of 40%. You're looking for investments, not trading vehicles. The Turnover tells you how much of the portfolio is bought and sold during one year.

Median Market Cap: $1 billion minimum, $10 billion maximum. You don't want to own very small companies internationally because the odds of success are much lower. Median Market Cap refers to the capitalization of the stocks the fund buys. The capitalization is determined by multiplying the number of shares of stock times the price.

Results Display Setting: Display info for: All Available. You want to see all the funds that match your variables and then rank them.

In this screen that I just described, the following funds met the requirements: None. That means the criteria were too confining for the search and need to be adjusted. That's the way screenings are. When you go for your ideal, you don't always find it. Then you start to fine-tune it to reality. And unfortunately, the only way to do that is to change one or two parameters and see if those are the ones that will give you results.

In terms of which parameters to work on first, remember that we're going for low-risk investing. So work with the Ratings parameters first, changing them by adding a little more risk. If there are still no funds that fit within your Comfort Zone parameters, then international investing doesn't belong in your portfolio. Use the same screening program for finding Growth Funds, Value Funds, Income Funds, etc.

More Screening Programs

There's an excellent one on MSN Money: http://moneycentral.msn.com/investor/research/fundwelcome.asp?Funds=1. It has four levels of screens: Top Performing Funds; Easy Screener; Deluxe Screener; Power Searches.

The first one, Top Performing Funds, is of mild interest. You can choose World Stock as your option and click on Go. It will return the best funds based on their performance over the last 3 months (no interest to us) and then show another list of funds based on their performance of the last 3 years, which also gives their performance over the last 5-years. This one is of more interest, especially when looking at the 5-year performance. But this is not a screen that lets you define the parameters.

The second option, Easy Screener, gives more information about the top 25 funds in the World Stock category, including: the name of the fund, its Front End Load (we want 0 here), the Expense Ratio (as close to 1 as you can find but tempered with the fund's performance; you may pay a little more in expenses for better performance), the 1-year total return (of some interest, but not much) and the all important 5-year annualized return, the most important number, the one that tells us, on average, what the fund made every year in the last 5 years. Remember, it's an average so the return for any one year may be way up or way down. The funds are ranked by their 1-year average return. What you'd like to find is a good return over the last year, and a great average annualized return for 5 years. When I did the screen research for this paragraph, the best fund was Oakmark Global, which had a 1-year return of 23.3% and a 5-year average return of 18.8%.

But don't buy this fund based on the information above, even if it shows up as the best performer when you do your screen. Only buy a fund after you have investigated it fully. The point here is that you want to look at the 1-year performance and the 5-year performance and pick the fund that has high returns for both, not necessarily the highest return in the 1-year column.

The third option is the Deluxe Screener, which requires the user to download a program from Microsoft. While it is a good program, it is more for the advanced investor.

The fourth option, the Power Search, offers two searches: Basic and Deluxe. The Basic Search returns funds in several categories, including World Stock Fund. By clicking on that heading, a list of top funds is shown, ranked by their expense ratios. It also shows the 1-year and 5-year returns as well as the front load. Each listing has the fund's name, its symbol, and a link to a description of the fund. When you click on the fund's symbol you go to a Morningstar page that gives a synopsis of the fund. This page is not enough information to base an investment on, but it gives you the basic information you need to decide if you want to spend more time investigating the fund.

The Deluxe Power Search requires use of the downloaded software to fully utilize its power.

More mutual fund screening programs are on these Web sites:

Forbes.com http://www.forbes.com/finance/screener/Screener.html

Morningstar http://screen.morningstar.com/FundSelector.html

Your brokerage firm has good information as well. Not all funds will be represented by every brokerage firm, but some of the online brokers such as Schwab, Ameritrade, Scottrade, and others have research tools that show the best funds in several categories, including international funds.

The Infinite Variety of Funds

Here are a few examples of the funds you can buy:

- Balanced funds, also known as hybrid funds, invest in stocks and bonds, with some cash holdings as well. Recommended for the Core Portfolio.

- A blend fund (also known as a core fund) invests in all levels of companies—small, mid-size, and large—and, unless prohibited by their prospectus, in growth and value companies.

- Bond funds buy debt instruments of companies and governments. They receive the income from the bonds as well as trade bonds for capital gains or losses. These tend to be less volatile than stock funds. Within the group there are Junk bond funds (also known as high-yield bond funds); treasury bond funds; treasury note funds; treasury bill funds; corporate bond funds; short-term bond funds; convertible bond funds, and many more.

- Global and international funds invest in stocks and bonds outside the United States.

- Index funds mimic a specific index such as the Nasdaq 100 or the S&P 500.

- Large-cap funds specialize in companies over $10 billion in market cap. Good choice for the Core Portfolio.

- Mid-cap funds focus on medium-size companies having a market cap between $5 billion and $10 billion.

- Money market funds always have a value of $1 and invest in very short-term corporate and government debt. Rates are usually higher than other short-term investments. It is a good place for cash while waiting to invest longer term.

- Sector funds invest in a specific industry such as health care, technology, energy, precious metals, etc. This is a great way to add a sector to the Core Portfolio.

- Small-cap or aggressive growth funds specialize in smaller companies, usually with a market cap of $1 billion to $5 billion.

- Value funds find stocks with low stock prices relative to their earnings or assets. These are also highly recommended for the Core Portfolio.

It's worth repeating: mutual funds are a great way to start investing. Spend time on the various sites with mutual fund screeners. Get familiar with the data presented. And here's one final tip: Vanguard Funds are known for their very low fees. Always check whatever fund you are considering against a similar fund offered by Vanguard. If the performances are similar, go with Vanguard. You'll have more of your money working for you because you'll pay lower or fewer fees.

2

Find Your Comfort Zone

You will do foolish things, but do them with enthusiasm.

—*Colette, French author*

I f you were to start swimming lessons, the first thing you'd need to know is which end of the pool is the deepest. You'd avoid it until you learned how to swim. The same is true for investing. Until you understand where the danger is, you can't get to your Comfort Zone.

The following mistakes are the deep end of the investment pool and carry the most penalties for investors. Avoid them and you'll improve your investment returns and eliminate many stressful days and nights worrying about your money. If you can discipline yourself to shun these, you'll be more relaxed about investing and well on your way to your Comfort Zone.

Nine Basics to Reach Your Comfort Zone

1. Never Buy a Hot Tip

This is probably the most common error. Every one of us has gotten a hot tip, a sure thing, a can't miss stock or real estate deal. We see a talking head on TV (in some cases a yelling head) and assume that: (a) the person wouldn't be on TV if they didn't know what they were talking about; (b) the stock or land recommended must be about to go up. If only we can get our "Buy" order in fast enough, before everyone else hears the same thing, we'll make a fortune.

Resist the urge. Count to 5,000 while you do a little research. If you're starting to invest, you don't know how to research stocks yet but you will by the end of this book, so hang in there. And as for real estate investments, those are for another book.

Never buy a hot tip. Whether it's from Warren Buffett, the best investor of all time, or a cab driver who's wealthy beyond imagination but can't resist the sound of the horns, don't do anything until you know a stock well.

Just because *they* love the stock shouldn't mean anything to you. Maybe they only have a few hundred shares. Maybe it's so risky that it will go out of business in three months if it doesn't get new financing, but if it does, it's straight up. Maybe it pays a large annual dividend to shareholders but hasn't moved in ten years.

It might be a great stock. Or it might be a stock they're trying to sell. Yes, Virginia, there are people who tout stocks they are selling just so there are more investors for them to sell to. It's called *Pump and Dump.* They pump up the stock with their hype, then dump it while everyone else is buying. There was a famous Fidelity Mutual Fund manager who did that. He no longer works there.

Most stock pickers on TV do know what they are talking about. They rarely are selling a stock that they recommend. But that doesn't mean they're touting the right stock for you. Until you've investigated it and know what it does, how expensive it is, and whether it fits into your investing goals, you are buying blind.

You will buy and hope for the best. That hope is what takes you out of your Comfort Zone. Knowledge about the stock will put you in it.

Never buy a hot tip. Investigate the ones that sound interesting. Be cautious on all of them. When you know enough about a stock that you're comfortable, know that it fits your objectives and your risk profile, then buy it.

2. Never Buy Too Much of One Stock

In investing, there's something called *Asset Allocation*. I'll cover it in depth later, but the basic idea is that you've got to buy a lot of different things so you don't put all your money at risk on one thing. Whether it's real estate, gold, stocks, or the horses, if you don't curb your irrational exuberance for that one thing, it will most likely wipe you out if it doesn't work out.

The problem with putting too much money in one stock or any one thing is that you watch it like a hawk and live or die with each up and down movement. You constantly hope it will go up and live in fear that it will go down. When it does lose value, you die a thousand deaths. Will it go back up? Will it go down further?

That doesn't make you comfortable. It only heightens your anxiety and takes you far away from your Comfort Zone.

A friend of mine recently asked for a hot tip. He said he needed one big hit before he retired. He wanted to put all his money in one stock. If it did well, he'd have it made. He was desperate enough not to finish the thought: If it didn't do well, he'd be broke. (I didn't give him a tip.)

That's what you want to avoid at all costs: losing large amounts of money. Even when you do a great job researching a stock and make sure that it has everything you want, then buy it at a great price, you can still get severely damaged. Ask the investors who owned MCI or Iridium or Enron or any other stock that went bankrupt because of illegal moves or ineptness by the management. It happens too often to ignore.

This doesn't mean you go to the other extreme and avoid stocks, but it does mean you have to be prudent at all times, never putting more into one stock than you can afford to lose. Hopefully, you will always gain. If you do, please call me. You'll be the first person in history to do it.

Never buy just one of anything. Diversify into many investments, never putting too much in risky ones that may go to zero. I'll describe how to diversify in chapter 5, "Sectors and Industry" groups. It's one of the keys to reaching your Comfort Zone and peace of mind.

3. Don't Always Enter Market Orders

A market order is a "buy" or "sell" order for a stock that you place with your broker. It tells the broker you are willing to pay whatever price the market is asking for a stock or willing to accept any price the market is bidding for a stock. In other words, you'll pay the going rate or you'll accept the current bid for a stock. This behavior will cost you money. Not one of our goals.

That's because the "market" for a stock is many times only good for 100 shares. The specialist on an exchange such as the New York Stock Exchange or the market makers that bid or offer stock on NASDAQ usually only have to make a market for 100 shares. Once they buy or sell 100 shares at the price they have posted, they can move that price down or up.

If you go in to buy a stock that doesn't trade very much (referred to as "thinly traded" or "illiquid") and want to buy 500 shares, you may end up paying much more for the stock than you think. That's because the market maker or specialist has the right to move the price up every 100 shares. Sometimes that upward movement can be surprisingly strong.

Let's say a stock only trades a few thousand shares a day (compare that to Microsoft, which trades 70 million shares a day, as of this writing). When a stock trades in that small a quantity, buying and selling can be difficult. (You can see the average daily volume on most stock quote programs on America Online or MarketWatch or Yahoo!Finance or MSN Money. I'll tell you how to find these later.) The price can move as much as 5 percent or more when a seller or buyer wants to do something that involves more than 100 shares. If you were to enter a "Market" order to buy 300 shares, you may receive 3 different prices. Each 100 shares would be at a different, higher price.

To avoid this problem, especially with thinly traded stocks, use an order called a "Limit" order. This order lets you put in the price *you* want to sell or buy a stock. You stay in control of the pricing. You stay in your Comfort Zone. If your price is not met, you won't buy or sell the stock. Or you may only buy or sell part of your order, but you will not be paying more for your buys or getting less for your sells when you use the limit option. (I'll go through how to physically buy or sell stocks in chapter 13.)

The only drawbacks to a limit order? Many times you'll end up buying or selling odd lots (an odd lot is any amount of stock less than 100 shares). And at times you won't buy or sell all the stock you want. Sometimes you won't buy or sell any stock because the stock is never offered at the price you want to pay or bid at the price you are offering. These are small prices to pay for buying or selling stock at your price.

Sometimes when a stock is moving very fast, you have to enter a market order or it will get away from you. But only do this with very liquid stocks (stocks that trade a large number of shares, preferably in the millions, every day). That way, the price won't move dramatically when your order is executed. If the stock usually only trades a few thousand shares a day but is moving quickly, let it go for the moment, watch it, then revisit it when it settles down. Putting in a Market Order with a fast-moving, illiquid stock can be a very expensive way to buy or sell a stock.

4. Don't Follow the Herd

One common emotion most humans share is a need to socialize. We want to be with other people. We want to be accepted. We want to do what others are doing. Nowhere is that more evident than in the stock market.

When it seems everyone is buying and the market is charging ahead, it creates a maelstrom effect, sucking in most investors. They feel a need to jump into the market, sending off "Buy" orders to their brokers, "at the Market," determined not to miss a rally. The same is true when everyone seems to be selling. Many investors sell whatever they have, not even knowing whether the news that has created the selling applies to their stocks. They just want out because everyone else is jumping off the bridge. So they send in their "Sell" orders "at the Market" again. Either buying or selling, they wind up losing money most of the time.

Don't follow the herd. One of the sayings on Wall Street is that bulls and bears make money. Sheep get slaughtered. Don't be one of the sheep. In fact, if you have the personality to go against the herd, to do the opposite of what most other investors are doing, you will make much more money. And you'll be in your Comfort Zone while other investors are still wondering why they're so anxious about investing.

5. Don't Abuse Margin

A margin account is a type of brokerage account that lets you borrow money, pledging the stocks you own as collateral. When you open a brokerage account, you have an option: you can open a "Cash" account or a "Margin" account. The cash account requires that you pay for all your stocks with cash. When you sell stocks, you will get cash back or you can leave the cash in the account to use for another purchase. Many investors only have cash accounts because they don't want the temptation of borrowing money against their stocks.

If you are sure you will never, ever need a short-term loan that's easy to get, or that you cannot resist leveraging yourself to the very limits of your creditworthiness, don't open a margin account. It will quickly take you out of your Comfort Zone. Borrowing too much money or buying too many shares of stock is a surefire way to create stress in your life.

Margin works a lot like your credit cards, only you use stock as collateral to borrow against. (If your credit cards are all at their maximum credit line, then don't even think about investing, much less using margin. Pay the cards off first.) If you have trouble restraining your credit charges, you'll definitely have problems controlling a margin account. But if you're like most people and can handle credit, seriously consider a margin account. Like any credit, open a margin account only if you can handle it.

When you have one, you can borrow as much as 50% of the value of your stocks that are eligible for margin. Most are. It's as easy as writing a check from the checking account that automatically comes with a margin account. Your brokerage firm takes care of the details. If you need some quick money at very good rates, this is a type of loan that makes sense, if you're going to pay it back very fast.

Or if you want to buy more stocks, you can buy as much as two times the amount of stocks that your money would buy in a cash account. That's because you can borrow money from your stocks to buy more stocks. This is not advisable for most people because when your stocks go down (and they will—as well as up), you will lose twice as much money. And you will be forced to sell your stocks to cover the dreaded "margin call."

A margin call is when your broker sends you a note in the mail saying that your account needs more money. In other words, you have to feed this margin beast when your stocks get too low in value. If you don't have the cash to add to your account, you can sell some of your stocks to settle the margin call. But then you're selling at a loss because they're down. In most instances, using too much margin forces you to sell when you least want to and will guarantee you lose money.

Margin, much like a Corvette, is not dangerous unless it's used foolishly. If used wisely, it can be of help to investors. A margin account gives you access to money in a very timely manner. For example, you may want to buy more stock than you would normally because you're convinced you've found a great one. In those instances, use margin sparingly with the vow that you will pay off the borrowed money quickly. Don't overuse margin. It can bury you when your stocks go down. It will definitely take you out of your Comfort Zone if abused.

6. Always Understand What You Own

One of the most basic requirements of investing is that you must understand what the company does when you buy its stock. If you don't know what it makes, what markets it competes in, or how it generates revenues, then you have no clue as to when to buy it or when to sell.

All of these elements of a stock are part of doing research. If you're a novice, you don't know where to begin to find this information. You will by the end of the book. Suffice it to say that unless you completely understand your stocks, you won't know if a news announcement from a company you've invested in is meaningful or not. Similarly, if there is general economic news, you won't know if it applies to your holdings. Ignorance is not bliss in the stock market. Know and understand your stocks before you buy them. That way you'll know when to buy or sell and what prices are cheap or expensive.

This seems so obvious that it should be unstated, but too many investors don't know anything about their stocks. They act on hot tips without knowing anything. Don't buy a stock unless you've got very good knowledge of it. A later chapter will tell you how to identify the great stocks. If you don't know your stocks, you can't be in your Comfort Zone.

7. Don't Put Too Much Money in Stocks

Stocks are one of the best investments you can make. Over time, they have proven to be better than bonds, real estate, gold, stamps, dolls, art, or cars. But they shouldn't be your only investment.

You need to spread risk out over many different types of investments, including bonds and real estate and whatever else you think will appreciate. A good rule of thumb is: Never put more money into stocks than you can afford to lose and never buy them if you need the money within three years. Some would argue for ten years.

Also—THIS IS IMPORTANT—never put money into stocks until you've paid off your credit cards. I mentioned this above but it's worth repeating. That's because the interest rates on credit cards are much higher (usually 18% or more) than what you can expect to earn from stocks (stock returns average about 10% a year). While the return on stocks is an average (meaning that in many years the return is less than 10%—or even negative), those interest rates on credit cards are real and rarely go down. It can be really stressful when your stocks go down and your credit card debt keeps going up. That's a double whammy that hits you way out of your Comfort Zone. It's worth repeating: Don't invest unless your credit cards are paid.

As to how much should go into stocks, it depends on how old you are. The older you are, the less you want in stocks because they have a higher degree of risk than many other investments. If you hit a bad spell in the market, it can take years before it recovers. The stock market, as reflected in the Dow Jones Industrial Average of 30 industrial stocks, was stuck around the 1,000 mark (that's right 1,000 as opposed to 10,000 as of this writing) between 1965 and 1982 and didn't break through in a meaningful way until 1983. If you had bought near the highs, in 1965, you would have waited almost 20 years for the market to do better.

While that was a rare time in the market and the following 20 years broke all records, it wouldn't be a surprise to see that flat market repeated. If you look at the peak of the market in 1929, it didn't stop going down until 1932. That, too, was an aberration that will hopefully never be repeated. But it could. And that's the point. Prepare for the worst in the market and hope for the best. That means putting only enough money in stocks that you can afford to lose. And never put in money you need within a short period of time.

8. Never Sell Too Soon

Investors will often buy a stock, make some money in it, then sell it thinking they've done well. Then they watch it climb and climb and climb. Just think if you'd bought Microsoft and sold after the first 10 points of profit were made.

It's only human to want to protect the gains made from a stock. Investors watched many of their gains turn to losses if they were in stocks from 1999 to 2003, especially in technology and Internet stocks. After the euphoria of the '90s, the reality of the new millennium hit hard. When you've experienced a meltdown of that magnitude, you begin to think only defensively. But that's shortsighted.

Great companies will have up and down years. Their stock prices will fluctuate and try the patience of any investor. But great companies continually increase their revenues and earnings. One quarter's poor results due to one-time events (called "extraordinary" in accounting parlance) is not a good reason to sell a stock. Nor is it a good reason to sell a stock just because it has gone up.

You sell a stock when you see that its "growth engine" has stalled, if it's a growth company, and you want growth in your portfolio. Microsoft is a good example. It is now so large that it's hard to imagine meaningful growth in sales or profits to justify a high valuation, the kind it carried all through the 1990s. It was a great growth stock, but it is now more of a defensive, mature company. It's still a great company, but it's not expected to grow at the fast rate it did previously. If you want a growth stock, you will find better examples than Microsoft. If you want a mature, cash-heavy company with a monopoly, Microsoft is for you. And that's fine, too. The point is that now Microsoft is a different type of stock than it was in the '90s.

You sell a stock if its dividend is in jeopardy, and you own it for income. You sell a stock because you own too much of it after all the splits it has made, or because it has risen well above reasonable valuations. You do not sell a stock simply because it has gone up.

Many stocks will rise in value and still be cheap. That happens when their earnings outpace their price movement. If a company is growing earnings at 15% a year and its stock is only going up 10% a year, then it is becoming cheaper even though the price is going higher.

Too often investors sell a stock because they need money and have only one winner. Everything else is underwater. They need the money now. (This underscores why you only invest with a time horizon of at least three years. If you need the money too soon, you almost always have to get out of stocks at the wrong time.) It's only natural to take profits instead of losses. But that doesn't make it right. Needing money and a stock's performance are not correlated. However, selling a loser is psychologically very difficult because it says you were wrong. Nobody said investing is easy.

But by selling one of your losers, you allow your winner to continue to grow. You also won't have to pay taxes on any gains. By selling the loser, you will generate a loss that can be applied to any future gains you make. By selling a loser, you are saying you were wrong about the investment. No one likes to be wrong. Too bad. Sell it and let your winners keep making money. As they grow in value, you will forget about being wrong. You will be back in your Comfort Zone.

9. Always Sell Soon Enough

Not selling a stock soon enough can happen when you have one that has done very well, and you don't want to let it go because you have to pay taxes on the gains. Or when you've got a loser in the portfolio, and you can't let it go. You are emotionally attached, convinced that the stock will rebound if only you hold it longer. You just need it to go up several points and at least then you'll break even.

If you can get out of this habit, you'll save large amounts of money. Hanging on to losers is one of the most common mistakes investors make. They believe the stock will turn around if they just hold on. It well might, but why?

If you can answer that question, you'll be able to make a better decision about selling the stock. Various events will turn a stock and move it higher. Some of them are:

- **Higher earnings than expected.** But the earnings have to be a positive surprise because investors following a stock will know analysts are expecting earnings at a certain level. Unless the earnings are higher than expected, they will already be factored into the price of the stock. Most of the time, an earnings surprise will help a stock. The exception is when the company forecasts a slowdown in revenues and earnings for the foreseeable future.

- **A new contract.** A large contract that has not been expected will always move a stock up. However, a highly anticipated contract, one that has been possible for several months or longer, will most likely already be factored into the stock's price. In fact, when a highly expected contract is signed, sometimes a stock will sell off. That's because the news has already been priced in and some investors will move on to other stocks. This is a good example of the Wall Street maxim: Buy the rumor, sell the news. Even when the news is good, stocks can go down because the news wasn't as good as expected or the price already reflected the positive event.

- **A buyout of the company.** Unfortunately, many buyouts don't move the stock back to the level where you bought the stock. But they are usually done at a price higher than for what the stock is currently trading. You have no choice when the company decides to sell. You can wait until the deal is done and accept the cash or exchange shares in the new company, or you can sell your stock and move on to another one.

- **An analyst upgrades the stock.** This may or may not help the stock. It depends on who the analyst is and what firm he or she represents. The large brokerage houses like Merrill Lynch or Goldman Sachs have real clout with investors. When they say buy a stock, it moves up. If the analyst is with a small regional firm, the recommendation may or may not make a difference. Most of the time it doesn't.

There are other reasons for a stock to move higher, but these are the main ones. Unless you have a suspicion that one of these good things will happen, you're only wasting your time and money holding on to a losing stock.

Some rules for selling:

- **If the stock moves down a certain percentage, say 10%, sell it.**
  I know one famous investor, William O'Neil, owner of *Investor's Business Daily*, who only lets a stock drop 8% and then drops the stock. You have to come up with a percentage that makes sense to you. This discipline forces you to get out of losers without taking too much of a hit.

- **If you bought the stock for a specific event and it doesn't happen.**
  Don't hang around or hope for another event to bail you out. (Again, there is no room for hopes in the stock market. Hope takes you out of your Comfort Zone.) Most likely, the hoped-for event won't happen. I owned a high-tech company that made products that allowed utilities to read meters without visiting homes. One large Italian firm bought the system. It was great while they were installing the millions of devices. Then a Dutch firm did a beta test with the program, but they didn't buy it. Then the Italian firm finally got every meter installed. There were no more announced companies using the system. Revenues dropped dramatically without new customers, and so did the stock. The time to sell was immediately after the Dutch firm dropped the program. Most investors, including me, did, but many didn't. They held on because they hoped other firms would materialize or the Dutch firm would come alive again. As of this writing, and 15 months after the bad news, nothing new or good has developed for the company. This stock reached $113 at one point based on its future promise. Now you can buy all you want at $7. When expected events don't happen, get out of the stock.

Here is another argument you'll hear about not selling soon enough: the stock has done so well that the taxes will be horrendous. In other words, those investors are letting taxes dictate their investment decisions. That's wrong. Taxes are down to their lowest level in decades (15% for long-term gains). Never let taxes get in the way of selling a fully valued stock. It's much easier to pay the taxes when you have profits than to watch your stock plummet and have no profits at all. Taxes, in a way, show you how smart you are to take some or all of your gains.

An investor is caught between these two extremes: sell too soon or sell too late. You can't ever sell at the top, but you can easily sell at the bottom. That's why you need to check the news on a stock often; daily is preferable, which is easy to do on the many Web sites that I'll describe later. You've got a mission impossible: Don't sell a great stock too soon but dump a lousy one fast. Nobody said investing is easy. If they did, they haven't done it.

A Few More Pointers

10. Don't Buy the Wrong Stocks in an Industry

When you develop a well-balanced portfolio, you have many different stocks in various industries. In fact, a good way to start a portfolio is to pick five industries and buy one stock from each group. Let's look at the auto industry as an example of an industry group.

If you start investing by buying an auto stock, buy the strongest auto manufacturer, not the one that is hoping for a turnaround or the one that may have the next great engine that runs on water or any other break-through technology that may or may not work. The reason: To paraphrase Napoleon, God is on the side of the strongest company. In other words, the strong get stronger until they don't anymore.

Think of GM in the '50s and '60s when it dominated the car business with about 50% of the market versus their share today of 26%. As of this writing, the auto manufacturer with the most momentum is Toyota with Toyota and Lexus brands. While they don't have the largest U.S. market share, they are the global leaders.

PLEASE NOTE: I am not recommending you buy Toyota. By the time you read this, things may have changed in the auto industry. In fact, they *will* have changed, but to what degree, I don't know. None of the stocks mentioned in this book is recommended to you to buy or sell. If you like a stock you read about, investigate it fully, know it well, understand it completely. If it fits your risk profile and your portfolio, then buy it.

Industry leaders are where you want your money, not the guys with ideas but no revenue or a small amount of revenue with lots of hope. Hope and ideas don't create profits that allow for growth or cash flow that generate dividends or stock buybacks. The strongest companies make the most profits. They lead their industries in new products or services. Their revenues grow every year. You want to be with the winners, not the stocks that may be winners or hope to be winners. After you've built a solid portfolio of winning stocks, you can take more risk. Initially, only buy the industry leaders. Owning leading companies is a large part of being in your Comfort Zone.

11. Don't Day Trade

The other day I got an e-mail from a reader. She said she only had a small amount of money and was thinking of either buying one stock or day trading. Which did I recommend?

As fast as I could, I wrote her that a mutual fund was her answer. I described mutual funds in chapter 1, so let's focus for the moment on that second option: day trading.

Day trading is when you buy and sell stocks (often the same ones during a single day) and try to make money. Don't even think about doing this at home. You don't have the experience. You don't have the tools. You don't have the knowledge, and the education is very, very, very expensive.

I know of no one nor have ever heard of anyone who could only day trade stocks and make a living at it. The odds are stacked against you in this game. The spreads (the difference between the bid and the ask prices— thoroughly explained later in the book) are often so wide on stocks that you won't see them move up or down enough to even cover that spread. The commission costs can mount up very fast even if you're using a low cost, online broker. If you do make a profit, you have to pay the same tax rate as income on it. (Stocks held for more than a year qualify for the long-term capital gains tax, which as of this writing is 15%. All other gains are taxed at your income rate.) If you make a loss, you can't trade that stock again for 30 days if you want to use the loss for tax purposes. This is known as the "wash rule," which the IRS has placed on all stock trading.

There are too many challenges for most people to overcome to make money at day trading. Don't do it. You'll lose money.

If you absolutely must do it, use a small amount of money. Lose it. Then get back to investing. Day trading is the farthest you can get from your Comfort Zone.

12. Don't Try to Time the Market

This is when you decide to get out of the market because you think it is going down. Or when you have fully invested because you're convinced the market is going up. Much like day trading, you can't do this.

You can't time the stock market. No one can. It moves in mysterious ways, and whether it will move up or down in the future is something no one can foretell.

On the day I'm writing this, a Tuesday, the market was down almost 80 points in the morning because of a record trade deficit. Later in the day, the Fed (the Federal Reserve System) released the minutes from its latest meeting. They showed the Fed was not as worried about inflation as most market participants expected. The market finished the day up almost 60 points. That's a move of 140 points from bottom to top. In one day. If you had been too pessimistic in the morning, thought you should get out and wait for a turnaround, you would have sold all your stocks at the low of the day, only to watch them turn around and finish with gains. The market moves too quickly to time it.

That doesn't mean you can't lighten up on some of your positions and be more risk averse at times. That's prudent in a treacherous market, especially during a time when interest rates are going higher. Stocks almost always decline when rates go up, so having a lighter position in stocks makes sense during those times. But being out of the market altogether never does.

Some people might argue, at this point, that if they get out of the market and have all cash, they would be in their Comfort Zone. But consider this: If they're sitting on cash, their anxiety will increase when the market moves higher, and they're not in it! This can lead to hasty decisions to get back into stocks so as not to miss the next big move up. After they've put money back into stocks, they often watch them drift right back down. They're once again out of their Comfort Zone. Being totally out of the market never makes you comfortable.

Why? Because any factor weighing on the market can change without notice. For example, interest rates, one of the strongest forces on the markets, may stabilize instead of going up, as everyone expects. In fact, interest rates have a way of doing the opposite of what most experts forecast. It's just the nature of the beast. Trying to time your entry and exit points based on interest rates, or any other factor, is a waste of time and certainly money.

You can't guess what the market will do. When everything looks the darkest, when there's blood in the streets, that's often when the market turns and heads straight up. If you don't own any stocks, you will miss the best part of a rally. And rallies occur in both up and down markets. Some stocks go up, even if the market is going down. If you do the research and have patience, one or more of your stocks may be an outstanding performer while the rest of the market deteriorates.

Rather than getting out of the market altogether, a better tactic is to become conservative in a down market. If you feel most comfortable being very defensive, then put your portfolio in stocks that are growing earnings and dividends in industries that are necessities such as drugs and groceries. Buy only one-third to one-half as many of those stocks as you normally would. Keep your investable cash (cash you don't need for three years) in a money market account, ready to move back into the market when you feel the time is right. Whatever you do, don't put all your money in cash and think you can jump in at the bottom, then sell your stocks at the top. No one can do that. Stay in the market, even if it's only with a minimum position. If you're not in the market, you won't get the benefit of the rallies that will surely come.

13. Don't Sell All Your Stocks and Buy All New Ones

This happens when you reach a certain level of frustration. You've watched your stocks go down and down and down. Or they stay flat while the rest of the market is rallying all around them. You want in on the action.

So you wake up one morning and make a decision. Out with the dogs and in with the winners! You put in your sell orders, take your lumps, and buy some other stocks, hoping for the best.

Here's what you've just done. You've paid a lot of commissions. You haven't researched how your companies are doing. Notice I didn't say stocks. It's the companies you own, represented by stocks, that need to be looked at. Too often investors focus only on the stocks. The stocks live in an almost separate universe, one that is influenced by the emotions of day traders and investors and mutual fund managers and institutional investors.

While management knows about these factors, it goes about its business, for the most part, focused on making money for its shareholders, not making Wall Street traders happy. Unless you know how well or poorly your company is doing, you have no basis for selling its stock.

You've also racked up more commissions when you buy. Every sale and every buy has a cost attached. Even if it's very low, when you sell several stocks, it all adds up, against you.

You also might have generated some losses that are unnecessary, losses that now need to be made up by your new stocks before you break even. The new investments may or may not do the job.

Doing something emotional like selling all your stocks and buying a new batch of them rarely makes money. Emotions will cost you dearly in the stock market. Try to keep them for other things like love, friendship, and animals. Emotional decisions are not part of the Comfort Zone.

14. Don't Think You're the Only One Who Knows

Imagine a mountain. Think of information about a stock as rain. Where does the rain hit the mountain first? At the very top, where the smallest portion is. You, as an individual investor, are thirsty for information, but you are on the bottom of the mountain. Way above you, at the pinnacle, sit the biggest money managers, such as those working for mutual funds, insurance companies, and hedge funds. They may be a small part of the mountain, but they are the wettest people in investing. They generate huge commissions for brokers.

On Wall Street, money doesn't talk. It screams. The money managers mostly scream, "Water, water, water." And Wall Street brokers make it rain information on them. They get it first, and they get it constantly. They never go thirsty.

You, on the other hand, can yell all you want, and like a tree falling in the forest, no one will hear. That's because your commissions pale in comparison to the big hitters. Even with the new Full Disclosure Act, which requires that all investors get information simultaneously, you won't get the news in a timely manner. Not because you can't; it's just that you won't get the phone call from the research analyst or salesman as soon as the wire is sent out telling everyone the latest development about a stock.

Imagine you're a salesman. You have to prioritize your time. Who would you call first: the institution that gives you millions in commissions or the individual who generates maybe a thousand dollars a year? That's how brokerage firms prioritize.

That doesn't mean the institutional and retail brokers don't get the same information simultaneously. But getting the information to institutional investors who follow the market all day is done by pushing a direct line to the institution. Most individual investors have regular day jobs that don't allow them to stay glued to CNBC or the ticker tape. Retail brokers trying to reach their clients with the information can take much longer because the client is in a meeting, traveling, or on vacation.

What it really means is that the distribution of information is not a fair, even playing field, no matter how much the SEC (Securities and Exchange Commission) tries to make it so. Professional investors are set up only for investing. Everyone else is doing something that doesn't involve the market. That makes it impossible for everyone to hear the same news at the same time. Accept this. Understand that you don't know *anything* that institutional investors haven't already dissected and either dismissed or acted upon.

That doesn't mean you can't act on information. There are plenty of inefficiencies in the market. And institutional investors are, after all—or at least are reported to be—human. They make mistakes like the rest of us. But they do get paid a lot of money to use their brainpower to find winners and dump losers. Don't be discouraged because you don't get news first.

But do consider the information carefully before you act on it. You're definitely not the first, or the only, investor to know it.

15. Don't Think This Will Go On Forever

Many investors get discouraged from stocks that continually go down, day after day, week after week, month after month. Who wouldn't? Or they get punch-drunk with stocks that keep going up and up and up. Being giddy puts you as much out of your Comfort Zone as being depressed.

Too often investors make an erroneous assumption: The current direction of the market will continue. While it seems that way, especially when stocks are going down, the market never, ever continues in the same direction. You could make an argument that it always goes up because since its inception it has improved remarkably. But tell that to investors who lived through the period of 2000 to 2003. That felt like an eternity, as every day stocks went lower and lower until the NASDAQ index lost 70% of its value. Many investors abandoned the market by the beginning of 2003, just as it turned around and had a powerful rally. The markets didn't recover anywhere near their losses, but there was a lot of money made from the bottom to the top of the recovery.

Nothing goes on forever, not good or bad. Too often, investors get lulled into depression or euphoria because the market has continued in one direction for a long time. It's during these periods you need to be extremely vigilant. While you can't predict the bottom or the top of a market cycle, know deep in your heart they are coming. Don't get too complacent, ever, about your stocks. Continue to monitor their news releases. Keep aware of the economic trends (much more on these later). Take some profits if your portfolio is getting out of balance with winners or certain stocks that are valued way too highly. Take some losses if you have some stocks that have dropped by the certain percentage you've decided on or if events that were the reasons for buying them haven't occurred.

Be vigilant. You might want to needlepoint that slogan on a pillow and put it on your couch so you always see it. Fortunately, with a computer, keeping up with your stocks and mutual funds and bonds doesn't take more than a few minutes a day.

Thinking that nothing but good times lie ahead or that bad times will never end won't make you wealthy.

16. Don't Buy Too Much Hype and Hope

Investors often see too many stars when they hear what a company *will* do. They quickly envision all good things happening, great profits for the company, and big money for themselves. That's rarely how it goes.

It's easy to understand the emotion. When a biotech company describes its mission and initial indications of success against a major disease, most of us take the leap of faith that the path to profits is straight and a little downhill. More often, the path grinds to a halt in a very short while and around the corner is a mountain we hadn't seen.

We all *want* the best to happen but more often it doesn't—for any variety of reasons. There is extreme competition in every field. You can be sure that if one company is working on solving a problem, at least ten others are as well. The question for the investor is to determine who will come up with the answer the fastest and be able to make money on it. Many times a company will develop a new drug or new product and lack the management expertise or capital to bring it to market. They sell out because they didn't have the staying power to make it to the finish line.

A great example was Iridium. This was a company of engineering brilliance. It invented a phone in the '90s that, for the time, was a breakthrough: It would work anywhere in the world, almost.

The company raised billions from selling stocks and bonds. Institutions, most of them very respected, put in the majority of the money. The company, once funded, launched satellites to establish a network for the phones. At that time, it was cutting-edge technology. The phones could be used everywhere.

Well, almost everywhere. They didn't work in buildings in New York, but the signal was loud and clear from an oil platform in the Indian Ocean. These "portable" beauties, initially, weighed ten pounds. And cost $10 a minute to use.

It was a classic case of great engineering with marketing and product problems. People who could afford these very expensive phones wanted to use them worldwide, starting in their offices. And they expected them to be light and small. The company went bankrupt and took some of my money with it. I bought the hype and hope. I now refer to the company, and sometimes myself, not as Iridium but as "You're an idiot."

I had lunch recently with a venture capitalist friend who specializes in technology. He said his biggest challenge is to understand the timing of new product acceptance. In other words, he knows technology but not when the public will be ready for it. He cited Bluetooth and nanotechnology as two recent developments that were very exciting but difficult to gauge. He wasn't sure when or if they would take off. By the time you read this, they may be part of everyday usage. Or they may be down there with Iridium. Or most likely, the jury will still be out.

So if the pros have trouble with the timing of new technology, even though they see the full potential, know that it is very hard for you, the new or somewhat seasoned investor, to be sure of what will be successful. Don't be blinded by possibilities, by the hype and hope. There is no hope in the stock market. There are only profits and losses.

This doesn't mean you don't buy some small amount of stocks that have great promise and no profits after you've established a strong, earnings-driven portfolio. But they should be a very small part of your investments. Too many great ideas turn into great losses.

Remember that the best pros for investing in technology are the venture capitalists, and their experience is that about one in ten is a home run. Many of their investments go bankrupt before they go public. If they can't average better than that, imagine your odds.

One of the best ways to avoid jumping into these stocks is to make yourself wait a day before you buy them. Give yourself a full day after you hear about the next great breakthrough to investigate the company and its competition, the potential it has, and the quality of the management. While the stock may move up from the day before, it may not. Or it may move down. If it's a great stock that delivers on its promises, it will continue to go up for a long time after you buy it. One day won't make a difference.

Now you've seen the deep end of the investment pool, you know what to avoid. Next we'll look at common myths that pervade investing. Buying into them won't get you to your Comfort Zone.

3

Common Myths and the Realities Behind Them

A fool and his money are soon invited everywhere.

—Anonymous

You hear a lot of things about investing. Some of them are true. But you also hear a lot of nonsense. Some of that nonsense has been passed along as truth, just as myth often is. The following myths are bunk.

Common Investing Myths

1. Penny Stocks Are Cheap

If I can convince you to never, ever buy a penny stock, I have done my job with this book. Penny stocks, as you might guess, sell for pennies. The fact that they sell for pennies should tell you something. But they're not even worth pennies. They're worthless 99% of the time.

The confusion here is between the *price* of a stock and the *value* of a stock. Just because something costs pennies doesn't mean it's cheap. Think of a watch that says Rolex on the face. If it doesn't have working parts or has very shoddy ones, then the watch is worthless. If you buy that watch for a few dollars on the street, you've wasted your money.

The same is true of penny stocks. They are merely shells of companies, often put together for the sole purpose of taking money from naive investors. They issue stock in a company that has no assets, products, or services. They write up a prospectus initially that promises some great breakthrough they're working on, such as a compound that cures cancer as well as leaves cars spotless when used as soap. Or sometimes the prospectus admits that they have nothing, that they are only pooling money together so they can buy a company or a product.

The unscrupulous stockbrokers who push these penny stocks have no conscience and will tell you anything to make you buy the stock. After all, for $1,000 you can buy tens of thousands of shares. Who wouldn't want lots of shares, especially if it's going straight up, just like the broker promised?

Penny stock certificates make good wallpaper, but that's the only benefit I can imagine. They will not go up after you buy them. If you try to sell them back to the broker, often times you won't even get a bid for them. If you do, you'll be shocked at how low it is. If you bought your stock for a nickel, don't be surprised if the bid is a penny. While that only sounds like a small amount, 4 cents, it is an enormous blow to your well-being. If you had 20,000 shares that you bought with your $1,000, you could sell them for $200 with that one-cent bid. Again, that's if you can get a bid. And don't forget there will be a commission added.

Avoid penny stocks. Hang up on brokers who have a strong urgency in their voices, pressuring you to get in now before the stock gets away. Please be rude to these people. It's the only way to discourage them. Ignore those "hot tips" e-mails. They are not selling real stock. Penny stocks are the most expensive kind you can buy. They will take you way, way out of your Comfort Zone.

2. Stock Splits Mean the Stock Will Go Up

This one happens often enough that it seems to be true. But it doesn't always happen. Sometimes stocks go down after a split.

First of all, most splits occur when a stock has moved up to a high price, many times close to $100 a share. The company announces that it will split the shares 2 for 1. That means for every 1 share of stock you own, you will receive 1 share of stock from the company. If you owned 100 shares you would receive 100 shares of new stock. It is put in your brokerage account automatically. After the split, you own 200 shares. You would have 2 times the number of shares after the split. Hence the name 2 for 1.

At the same time you are getting your shares, the stock is splitting its price in half. That is, the price does the exact reciprocal of what the shares do. If the split is 2 for 1, then the price goes down by one-half. When you look at your overall wealth, it is exactly the same after the split as before it. The only difference is that you have twice as many shares. The value of the company hasn't changed at all. The value of your stock hasn't changed.

Another way to look at this is to imagine a whole pie sitting on the table. The whole pie is now in one piece. If you take a knife and cut it exactly in half, you have two pieces of pie, but you still have the same amount of pie. Nothing has changed but the number of pieces. The same is true with stocks. They can be split, but nothing of their intrinsic nature has changed, only the number of outstanding shares that represent the same company is different.

So the stock split, in and of itself, does not have anything to do with whether a stock will go up or not. What makes a stock move is earnings. Stocks that enjoy higher prices usually have good earnings. Therefore, when there is a stock split in a strong-earnings stock, sometimes there will be a push up in the price after the split.

That's because the new price will attract new investors who didn't want to buy a stock that carried a high price. Some of them can't buy 100 shares of a $100 stock. So they ignore the stock. But if the stock is split in two, to $50, this price level will attract more buyers, simply on price. And that is the intent of the company.

The company splits a stock because it will attract more investors, thereby increasing the universe of owners. With a wider group holding a stock, it will often create support for a stock, meaning that there are more buyers waiting for it to go down when sellers come into the market. A lower-priced stock is easier for the public to buy. The company hopes that by splitting its shares, it will attract more buying interest.

You will see some stocks rally after a stock split, but not always. Don't think you have to immediately buy a stock the moment it announces a split. It may be a great stock and move higher after the announcement, especially if a number of new investors buy it after the price becomes more attractive. But don't ever buy a stock simply because it's going to split or has recently split. If it's a good investment, with all the right attributes (which you will learn in chapter 7), then buy it.

But not all high-priced stocks (I don't mean overvalued stocks, but those that have a high absolute price) will split. One of the best stocks over the last 30 years has been a company run by Warren Buffett called Berkshire Hathaway. It's a conglomerate of many different companies from See's Candy to GEICO insurance. It trades for $82,500 a share as of this writing. That's down from $94,000 per share within the last year. The stock has never split nor will it as long as Mr. Buffett runs the company. He doesn't believe in stock splits because they don't create any value, for the company or the investor. If you had done your research ten years ago and recognized the quality of the company, you could have picked up one share for $22,000.

If you wait for a split to buy a stock, to put it in a price range you like better so you can buy more shares, you may miss a great opportunity. If you had purchased just one share of Berkshire ten years ago, you would have made $60,500. Volume isn't the key to success in stocks.

Again, stock splits don't do anything for the value of the stock or your portfolio. All they do is increase the number of shares.

3. Stocks Return 10% a Year

You will often hear this quoted. Experts will cite studies that show stocks are the best investments and average 10%-a-year returns. The key here is that the 10% is an average over a long period of time. If you take the wrong periods of time, you will show losses. However, over decades, stocks have always performed well, as reflected in the Dow Jones Industrial Average, which has gone from a value of 41.2 in 1932 to a high of 11,497 in 1999. That's an increase of 27,805%. Of course, it hasn't been straight up since the 1930s.

There have been plenty of years when stocks were down. Or years when stocks were flat. In those years it was little comfort to quote averages of 10% growth.

What's important to remember about this particular myth is that the direction is correct but not the absolute number. In other words, over time, stocks do go up (again, in a broad sense). But individual stocks do whatever they want. They have no correlation to the averages. It's no comfort to investors if they hear the Dow is up 50 points in a day if their stocks are down. In fact, it makes the hurt even worse. It feels like everyone else made money on that day except them.

Some great stocks have given a 10% average return over a long period of time but they've done it in spurts. After the initial surge in price, they often settle back. Sometimes they go down for a while because investors have bid up their prices beyond realistic expectations. Sometimes their prices flatten for months or years as earnings catch up to the price.

The point here is to have realistic expectations. That's a key to being in your Comfort Zone: realistic expectations. Over decades, with the right stocks, you may average 10% a year. But don't count on it just because there's a myth that says that's the return you should expect.

4. Insiders Are the Best Indicators

The term "insiders" refers to people who have knowledge of a company at the highest levels. Insiders are all the officers of a firm as well as its board of directors. These people know what the company will do, and they have the authority to make the company move in one direction or another.

Insiders have to file with the SEC (Securities and Exchange Commission) every time they buy or sell stocks. That way, the public knows what these influential people are doing. If you are already assuming that an insider selling means they want to get out before there is bad news, you're wrong. (It might mean that, especially if all the insiders are selling at the same time and in large quantities. That would be a concern.)

But insiders sell for many reasons. We'll get into that, but first you should know about something called a 10b-5-1 filing. This particular SEC document is usually filed well ahead of any sales that an insider makes. This filing tells the world that the insider is selling a certain number of shares automatically at certain times. In other words, no matter where the price is, no matter what the news moving the market or the stock, this insider is going to sell stock.

Insiders use this method of selling because it takes away any questions investors might have. By declaring that they are selling every quarter or every month or other stated interval, a certain number of shares, it tells the world that they are not trying to time the market or take advantage of any news about the company.

As mentioned earlier, there are many reasons for an insider to sell stock. Chief among them is portfolio diversification. Most insiders purchase stock years before their company has gone public. They have been waiting a long time to be liquid again, to have use of that money. If the price of the stock has moved up nicely, they can sell some of it to pay for things like houses, cars, divorce settlements, taxes, or any number of things. They can also take the money and buy other stocks or investments, thereby diversifying their assets. These are by far the most common reasons for insiders to sell.

Just because there's an announcement that an insider is selling stock isn't enough information for investors. They have to look at the type of selling (for example, is it a 10b-5-1 sale?) as well as the amount. Usually insiders only sell a small percentage of their holdings at any one time. They, like you, believe in the company and want to participate in an ever-appreciating stock. In fact, you always want to look at how much stock insiders hold, which is easy to do on Yahoo!Finance. The more they have, the more of their fortune is tied in with yours.

What should raise a red flag of concern is the size of the sales and the number of insiders selling. If all the officers and directors are selling most or all of their holdings, you'll definitely want to get out of the stock. There is no stronger sell signal than that.

The other side of sales, however, is the buys. There's only one reason an insider buys company stock: because of a strong belief that the company will be doing better. When you see many insiders buying a large number of shares, there is a strong possibility that the company will be doing good things in the near future. This is not an absolute. Anything can happen that might prevent a positive outcome, but insider buying is always a good thing.

To put an even finer point on it, when officers in particular are buying, especially the president, chief executive officer or the chief financial officer, that's a strong indicator that good things might be coming. That's because these are the people who make things happen. They make the decisions and carry them out. While it's interesting if the board members are buying, they are not in the day-to-day decision making of a company. They are not the ones who execute the business plan. The officers do, and when they're buying in large amounts, that's a very good sign.

To track insider selling or buying for a particular stock, go to Yahoo! Finance and put in the stock symbol. When the quote is returned, look on the left side of the page. Click on the link that says Insider Transactions under the heading of Ownership. The link to the site is http://finance .yahoo.com. You can also find this same information directly at the SEC site (www.sec.gov) or at most major financial Web sites. (Later, I will go over many of these Web sites and give the URLs.)

Insiders can be a good indicator of possible stock movement, but only if the buying or selling is done in an extreme manner. Just because one or two officers or directors sell a small percentage of their holdings or buy a few thousand shares doesn't give an investor any real information for buying or selling the same stock. Don't blindly follow the insiders when they're buying or selling in small amounts. It usually doesn't signal anything of significance for investors.

5. Inside Information Is a Sure Way to Make Money

No, it isn't, but it's a sure way to go to jail. Ask Martha Stewart about that. Though she was never convicted of using insider information, it was her sales of Imclone stock that led to the entire fiasco. Those sales seemed to be triggered by information that her then-friend and chairman of Imclone told her.

What is inside information? It's any information from a company that hasn't been distributed to the general public. In other words, if you know the treasurer of a company and invite her to dinner, and she tells you that tomorrow earnings will be announced that will be better than expected, that's inside information. No one but you has been told of this positive surprise. If you were to buy the stock the next day, before the earnings were announced, you would be breaking the law.

There is a new law called the Full Disclosure Act (referred to as Reg FD for Regulation Full Disclosure). It requires that everyone must have the same news simultaneously. What this law does is make it harder for research analysts to get information from company officers so they can write reports for investors. Company management is reluctant to talk about anything that won't be publicized to everyone at the same time, because if they inadvertently say something to the brokerage research analysts that is determined to be "material"—something that would influence the price of their stock—then they'll be fined or go to jail because not everyone heard the same information at the same time.

In a way, the reality of the law is in exact contrast to its purpose since less information is being generated for investors. More and more companies make it a policy to not say anything to anyone about the future of a company. They don't know how the information will be construed, especially by the federal authorities. If the feds deem it to be meaningful and it wasn't given to everyone at the same time, then management is in trouble.

When there is information for everyone, it is usually released over a news wire service such as PR Newswire or Business Wire. The same news release, if it's newsworthy, will be broadcast over the Dow Jones News Service as well as radio and television stations. You will see it under a stock quote on most quote services on the Web. Many of these Web sites will send any releases about a particular stock for free if you sign up for the service.

Even with the new full disclosure rules, inside information is passed around. But it is less frequent, and the penalties are much harsher. There isn't an executive in the country who isn't aware of the penalties for giving out news to a friend or relative before everyone else gets it. So the playing field is getting a little more even. Inside information is getting rarer and rarer.

But the reality is that inside information isn't all that helpful to an investor. Many times, the news isn't that influential on a stock. Or the same information that an investor or a corporate officer thinks will be positive is seen as a negative by the market in general. Don't think inside information is the key to wealth. Nowadays it's more likely the key to a jail cell. Don't seek it out and if you ever hear it, don't use it. Nothing will take you farther from your Comfort Zone than having a roommate known as Big Daddy.

6. There's Always a Summer Rally

This is like saying there's always snow in December. For the most part that is true, if you live in the northern parts of the United States. But it's not always true, even in those states.

Predicting the stock market is much like predicting the weather. You look at past years and expect the same this year. Like the weather, the stock market doesn't know about the past.

What this old saying refers to is the fact that *many times* in the past there has been a rally during the summer. There isn't a scientific reason for it, but more summers than not, the stock market will have a rally during June, July, or August, though August is usually the slowest trading month in the market because of vacation time. Having said that, it was in August of 1982 when a huge rally started that lasted for years. Again, anything can happen at any time.

Just think about it for a second. If this summer there were events that made investors turn away from the market, such as a terrorist attack or a war or large increases in interest rates, there isn't going to be a summer rally, period, no matter what this myth suggests.

What does make a little more sense is the usual occurrence of a January rally. That's because January starts the new year, and many investors will put money in their Individual Retirement Accounts (IRA), which in turn will be invested in the stock market. Furthermore, many investors will take a fresh look at their portfolios and make changes, wanting to start a new year with new stocks. Finally, December is the month many investors sell their losing stocks for tax purposes but can't buy those same stocks back until 30 days later. That's because of the wash rule described in chapter 2. All of these factors make a January rally a lot more likely than a summer one.

The point is that investors can't count on a summer rally or even a January rally. In the past, there have been summers and Januarys when rallies have occurred, but that doesn't tell you anything about this upcoming summer or next January. If you want to have the odds on your side, then take into account the fact that many times there are rallies in these months. But don't think they happen every year at the same time. Investing simply isn't that predictable.

The media make a big deal out of these two time periods, always suggesting that rallies will be coming because it's a certain time of the year. Ignore the media on this one.

7. Stock Charts Can Tell the Future

It's hard to imagine that intelligent people believe they can look at a chart and determine where the price of a stock will go next.

A chart is an historical record of the price and volume of a stock. You can find a chart on any stock on most quote services on the Web. You'll see that prices go up and down for a stock. The chartists will try to convince you that you can predict where the stock will go based on this price history. You can't.

If anyone tries to sell you on this idea, here's a test. Print out ten charts for ten different stocks. Cut the charts exactly in half vertically. Throw them on the floor and have the chartist match the correct halves to form the whole chart. They can't do it. No one can.

That's because, once again, stocks don't know where they've been. They don't care where they've been. They only react to future events, not past ones. But that doesn't mean that these charts are a complete waste of time.

In fact, they can be very helpful to investors who have gathered "fundamental" research. Fundamental research is the kind that uncovers earnings, revenues, ratios—all the basics needed to judge a stock's value. The father of fundamental analysis was Benjamin Graham, who was Warren Buffett's mentor. His book *The Intelligent Investor* cannot be recommended highly enough. If you want to really understand a stock and the stock market, read this book.

Where charts can be of use is in determining an entry price for a stock. If you are convinced you have found a good stock with all the attributes that give it a strong chance of going up, you may find the final piece to the puzzle of when to buy the stock by looking at a chart.

The chart will show where the stock has previously hit a low price, then bounced up. If your stock is at or near that price level, there is a good chance the stock will once again find what is called "support" at that price. In other words, investors have come in to buy the stock at that price before, giving it support.

That doesn't mean the stock will go up again when it gets to that price. Remember the company has evolved since the last time that price was hit. If the company has gotten much stronger, and your research shows that marked improvement, there is a better chance it will go up. Buying the stock near the old low may be a good move, with the understanding of the possibility that the support that was there before may not materialize. If it doesn't, the stock will break through that old low and head further south.

The charts shouldn't dictate your buying and selling. They can be of help in seeing where a stock has been. They won't tell you where it is going. How can they? It makes no rational sense. How can a chart know that a contract will be signed or that an expected contract wasn't consummated? Don't spend a lot of time on charts. They don't hold the key to investing success or your Comfort Zone.

8. Stock Buyback Programs Mean the Stock Will Go Up

Many times a company will announce that it is going to buy back a stated number of shares or a certain dollar amount of stock. Most of the time the announcement comes when a stock price is low, and management wants to give a boost to the price. By buying in shares, the company, at least theoretically, is adding a strong buyer into the market, willing to absorb shares for sale. That will sometimes help hold a stock's price. Furthermore, after the shares are bought, those shares are either retired or they can be used for stock that is needed when employees exercise options to buy company stock.

If the stock is retired, that's good. It means there are fewer shares outstanding. With fewer shares, earnings will improve on a per share basis. That's because there are fewer shares to divide into the pool of earnings at the end of each quarter. Fewer shares mean higher earnings per share.

Many investors get excited about a stock buyback announcement. They believe the company is going to immediately go into the market and start buying stock. Nothing could be further from the truth.

Here's a fact about stock buybacks (also known as repurchase programs): Companies can announce them but they don't have to actually buy anything. Most announcements have no time limit on them, and there is no mandatory requirement that any stock be bought. In fact, most announcements read something like this:

"The Very Big Company announced today that it will buy back its stock. The price has gotten to a level where management believes it represents the best investment the company can make. The shares will be bought from time to time in the open market when the management believes the price is most attractive."

If you parse that, you'll see that there is no price target for where it will buy the stock. There is no time specified for when the purchases will be made. This is purely intentional. Sometimes this will help the stock price but not very often.

There are some announcements that are more specific, and they will help a stock's price in the short run. For example, if a company announces that it will be buying back $200 million of its own shares within the next quarter, without any stipulation as to discretion on the part of management, then that will usually help the stock, unless the stock has so many shares outstanding that even that amount isn't of consequence.

When you see a company announce a stock buyback, read the news carefully. Does it contain specific details as to when the buyback will occur or how much within a certain period of time will be bought? The more information that pins the management to action, the more likely the stock's price will improve. But even with those buybacks, don't expect large improvements in the stock. Buybacks aren't the answer to most stock ailments, especially when many of them are simply announcements with no action behind them. Ailing stocks need earnings for their prices to go higher.

9. To Make Real Money, You Have to Buy IPOs

IPO stands for Initial Public Offering. Everyone's heard stories of hot IPOs that doubled in a day. If only, if only, we all say. Forget about IPOs, for two reasons.

First, you won't get any of the good ones. The best IPOs are given to the best customers. The more commissions a broker makes from a client (and these are all clients, not just individuals), the more of an IPO stock that customer can buy. It doesn't mean that an institutional investor will get as much as it wants, but at least it will get some of it. Really "hot" IPOs can sometimes be parceled out in lots of 100 shares. No one is happy, but at least they get something. IPOs are just like the "rain" of information described earlier. The top of the mountain gets the most. You are not an institutional client. You will not get a hot IPO.

Another reason it's so hard for individuals to buy an IPO is that only the underwriting broker and the selling group have shares to sell to clients. The underwriting broker is the broker that is bringing the stock public. The name is on the left side of the "tombstone" (a paid ad in *The Wall Street Journal* that looks something like a tombstone) that announces the deal. The selling group is the names below the underwriting broker, also known as the lead manager. Some of the largest firms, like Goldman Sachs, won't even take individual accounts with less than $1 million in assets. Most individual investors don't have that kind of wealth. As you might guess, Goldman gets a lot of the "hot" deals.

If you haven't gotten the picture quite yet, let me paint it in bright red: Money roars on Wall Street. The largest clients are given the best opportunities, the most research, the nicest dinners. It's the way it works. Having said that, don't think you can't make money by investing. There's plenty of opportunity for that. I'll show you how. Just keep reading.

There's another way to interpret what IPO means: It's Probably Overpriced. That's the second reason for avoiding these. While there are some spectacular IPOs that fly right from the start, there are many that never get off the ground. In fact, many of them go into the ground.

Very few stocks are priced correctly as an IPO. It's mostly science, but there is some art as well. As smart as the Wall Street investment bankers are, they can never be sure that an initial price is right for a stock. The only true determinant for a stock's price is the marketplace. When the stock starts to trade in the open market, investors will let the company know if they've put the price in the right place. Many times a stock is overpriced, and investors let the company know by selling the stock.

IPOs are not for most individuals. While there is a new process called the Dutch auction IPO, it is still unclear how well investors will respond to it. This process allows anyone to bid for the IPO at any price. A price is chosen that will sell all the shares being offered by the company. In that way, all shares will definitely sell. If you bid above the price, you will buy your shares at the lower price that cleared all the shares. If you bid less than the clearing price, you don't buy any.

This process seems to work well for small- to medium-sized companies. It's hard for them to raise capital through the Wall Street giants because they're not large enough to produce enough fees for the large firms to bring them public. But the Dutch auction is a direct challenge to the normal Wall Street way of doing business in IPOs. The big established firms don't like it. (That alone should raise your interest in the process.) They want it to fail so they can continue their monopoly on IPOs and allocate the good ones to their best clients. That way the best clients will come back and do more business with them. It's a very nice circle, for Wall Street and the big clients. You, however, are not in the circle.

The Dutch auction for IPOs is interesting, but it hasn't been around long enough to see if it will dent much of the IPO business. Google famously went public this way and put the auction process in the public's eye. (As of this writing, Google is selling for $405 a share versus its auction price of $85.) Morningstar and Overstock.com went public this way as well, though neither enjoyed Google's success. Time will tell if more IPOs will be done this way. If they are, it will give individual investors an opportunity to participate.

Don't be too anxious to buy them, even if it's a Dutch auction, unless you can buy them at your price. As mentioned, it's only after the stock has traded for a while that a price level is determined that represents fair value for the company. Sometimes that price is higher than the IPO. Sometimes it's lower. If you're going to buy any of them, be sure you read the prospectus extremely well and understand what it is you're buying and the price you're paying.

Here's the way the pros evaluate an IPO. First they put the new stock in its industry group. As an example, let's use a theoretical stock called Almost National Bank (ANB), a large regional bank that offers mortgages and business loans. This stock would most naturally fit into an industry group called Regional Banks. Now the pros compare all the relevant data points for Regional Banks to our new ANB issue.

For banks, the most commonly used valuations are Price to Earnings Ratio (P/E), and Price to Book Value (P/B). While there are many other valuations to consider, these two tend to dominate where a bank stock trades. These two are the first ratios investors will look at when a new bank has an IPO.

You can find these two ratios at various Web sites as well as the comparative ratios for the industry. I'll use Yahoo!Finance in this example. Go to http://finance.yahoo.com. Enter a symbol for a regional bank. I'll enter the symbol for Zions Bancorp (ZION), a regional bank in Salt Lake City.

As an aside, because the symbol has 4 letters, it means the stock trades on the NASDAQ. If a stock has less than 4 letters, it most likely trades on the New York Stock Exchange, though a few trade on the American Stock Exchange. NASDAQ stocks are traded by market makers that are not located on a central exchange. They are individual brokerage firms that post bids (the buy side of the market) and offers (where stock is offered for sale). If a stock trades on an exchange, it is handled by a specialist, one firm, that makes the market offers to buy and sell in the stock.

Back to our bank. By entering the symbol ZION, I can get a current quote that is the price the stock sold at last. That price is about where you can expect to buy or sell the stock. The bid side of the market is where you would sell it; the offer side is where you would buy.

On the left side of the Web page, where I'm viewing the stock quote on Yahoo!Finance, are several links. Under the heading of "Company," there is a link called "Competitors." By clicking on that link, the page changes to a listing of several banks that are in the same category as Zions. In this case, there is a row with Bank of America, Wells Fargo, and Washington Mutual. The last column of information is entitled Industry. That's the one we want.

This column shows what the average is for each ratio in the regional banking industry. The one we want is the P/E ratio. It's the third to the last entry and as of this writing is 16.11. We will want to compare what ANB's P/E ratio is to this number.

The next data point we need to find is the Price to Book Value (P/B). This is simply the price of the stock divided by the book value, the measure of how much equity is in a firm. The equity is what a stockholder owns. The P/B is located in the link called Key Statistics, which is on the left side of the same Web page. By clicking on it, you go to a page of numbers. The fifth entry down is the Price to Book. In this case, it shows Zions to be 2.23. Unfortunately, Yahoo!Finance doesn't show the industry average (neither do AOL or any of the other free databases on the Web.) So you just have to do a little calculating on your own.

By looking up the P/B for each of the banks mentioned above (you simply put in the symbol for each stock in the box to the right and above the statistics showing for ZION), we find that BAC (Bank of America) has a P/B of 1.84, WFC (Wells Fargo) shows 2.62, and WM (Washington Mutual) shows 1.65. Now add up those 4 numbers (including 2.23 for Zions) and divide by 4. That would give you an average P/B of 2.08.

This is too small of a sample to say that the industry average is 2.08, but it gives us a good idea of about where the average most likely is. It might be a little higher or lower, but because these are such large regional banks, they would represent the industry well.

So what do we know now and why do we need to know it? We know that the average P/E ratio for regional banks is 16.11 and the P/B ratio is 2.08. We take these two data points and compare them to our IPO stock that we're considering and see what its P/E and P/B ratios are. If the IPO is going to attract a lot of money, it will most likely have to have a P/E and P/B lower than these two averages (lower because it will be cheaper than the existing stocks in the same group, making it more attractive to investors). If it doesn't, most investors will buy other, existing regional banks unless there is something unique about Almost National Bank that makes it more valuable than other regional banks. Most likely there isn't.

This is exactly the process that investment bankers use to price new issues. Of course, they add a lot more companies into any average they use and have more data points to consider. But this is a good start for any investor who wants to value an IPO. Get the industry averages for several ratios and then compare them to the IPOs ratios, which are given in the prospectus or can be easily calculated. If the IPO isn't cheaper than the existing competitive stocks, buy one of those instead of the IPO.

Some IPOs are unique. That's why they're successful. In this case, putting them in the same industry group that is "close" to what they do isn't going to put the correct valuation on the IPO. But investors have to start somewhere. Even if an IPO has a niche that no other company competes in, do your evaluation against the nearest industry group. It's not perfect, but it gets you some real numbers to work with.

Again, investing in an IPO isn't necessary to make money in stocks. In fact, the game is rigged so that great IPOs go only to the largest investors unless it's a Dutch auction IPO. But the Dutch auction process has been slow to gain traction. While the Google IPO made investors aware of it, there has not been a groundswell of new issues following it, as of this writing. That might change.

Even if you're looking at a Dutch auction IPO, use the same valuation technique I've described. Find out the industry averages for several valuation ratios such as P/E and P/B or Price to Sales (P/S), and compare those to the same ratios for the IPO issue. You'll have a much better chance of buying it at the right price if you know what industry averages are. If you can't buy it at your price, at least you've established the level where you would purchase the stock. By tracking how it trades, it may get to your price, giving you an opportunity to buy it later. In any case, you made your investment decision on facts rather than feelings, a position of strength and comfort when investing.

10. Wall Street Analysts Pick the Best Stocks

Totally incorrect. Wall Street analysts pick the stocks that will generate the most commission for their firms.

Here's how that works. An analyst is a highly paid, intelligent professional who writes research reports on companies. The question you have to ask is: How are the companies chosen?

The stocks that usually get coverage are the ones that the firm has brought public, also known as underwritten. As part of their commitment to a new company, most brokerage firms will have an analyst write research on the company going public. That's part of what the new company is paying for in the commissions it pays for the IPO (usually 7% of the total equity amount raised—that's why you don't pay any commission on an IPO; it's paid by the issuing company).

The analyst will issue a report or two and see how much trading is done in the stock after it is public. If there isn't much interest in the stock, the brokerage firm will most likely drop its coverage because there are no buy or sell orders coming through to pay for the analyst.

If that is the case, then the analyst will turn his or her attention to other stocks in the same industry, especially the ones where the brokerage firm wants to get new business for the investment banking department of the firm. By writing up the company, analysts get access to the firm's officers to ask questions. If a rapport develops, or the reports are very positive, the company just might give the next capital markets deal to the firm where the analyst works.

While there has been an increased focus on the separation of research and investment banking, this is how the Street works. The investment banking department is where the big fees are made. They need a competitive edge because the large stock and bond deals are fiercely sought after. If a brokerage firm can get an advantage by using their analysts to gain entry to officers of a company thinking of doing a deal, they will. So they use their analysts sometimes as a beginning point of a dialogue between the company and the brokerage firm.

That's why it's very hard to find out much about small, publicly traded companies. No analysts follow them because there isn't enough stock traded, nor are there any investment banking deals for a brokerage firm to pursue. In other words, the company isn't big enough to warrant attention because it doesn't generate commissions from its stock or investment banking fees from issuing equity or debt.

That leaves the larger companies with lots of stock to trade and deals to do. It's not uncommon to find 15 to 30 analysts covering a large stock. As of this writing, Microsoft has 23. IBM has 17. Intel has 27. These are big companies no matter how you measure them, their shares are widely held, and there's plenty of business for Wall Street. So the analysts get assigned to them and the research reports get written.

So that's where analysts' recommendations from brokerage firms come from, for the most part. While there has been some change in the way stocks are covered since the 2000 tech crash put the spotlight on analysts' reports, it has not been dramatic. The stocks covered aren't necessarily the best stocks, nor are the reports objective because a negative report will put the brokerage firm down the list for possible deals and/or the analyst will have a hard time getting access to management after a bad word has been uttered.

One good way of not being swayed by brokerage firm reports is to use a third-party source. The best one available to every investor is Value Line. Almost every library in the country carries this helpful publication, usually in the reference section. It covers 1,700 stocks with an objectivity that brokerage firm analysts can't have. While it doesn't have the depth of many analysts' reports, it does give plenty of data, as well as an opinion of whether to buy, sell, or hold a stock. I can't recommend this publication too highly for beginning investors. You may find it so useful that you'll eventually subscribe.

Don't think analysts from Wall Street firms give objective advice on a stock or that they are only recommending the best stocks. Their goal is to make customers buy or sell more stock and to help their firms do more business with companies they cover.

11. Bigger Is Safer

No it isn't. Too often investors think a large stock is one that won't have problems; that it has some special shield that prevents bad things from happening. Sometimes investors think because a stock trades on the New York Stock Exchange there is some extra measure of safety attached to it. There isn't. Or that because a stock has passed the scrutiny of the Securities and Exchange Commission (SEC), which all have to do before going public, that the stock has been blessed in some way, making it safer. It isn't.

Here's how the process works. Before a company, large or small, can go public, it must file a great deal of information with the SEC. The SEC then has its lawyers and analysts look over the documentation. The only thing it is looking for is full disclosure of material information that an investor would need to make a judgment on the company's stock. They don't care what the company did (as long it wasn't illegal), whether it made money or lost it, never opened for business, or whatever other negative factors you can imagine.

The SEC only cares that investors have been told about it. In other words, the SEC isn't there to determine if the company is good or bad at what it does; it's there to make sure that the company tells everyone exactly what it is doing. The investor needs to decide whether it's good or bad. The SEC does a great job of going over numbers, tallying them, comparing them, etc. If there are mistakes in the numbers, they get corrected. You can be sure the numbers are right when you look at a prospectus.

The prospectus is the document that every investor has to receive when buying an IPO. You can get what is called the "red herring" before the IPO (it doesn't have the price on the cover). The name comes from the red ink used in parts of the prospectus. After the IPO, you get the prospectus, with the pricing. The red herring will have everything the prospectus does except the price. So an investor has plenty of good information on which to base an investment decision. But the SEC has only cleared the information for its truthfulness, not for its merits as an investment. You have to do that yourself.

The IPO can then start trading on the NASDAQ or the New York Stock Exchange (NYSE). Each has a set of listing requirements that have to do with the size of the company's revenues, assets, and shareholders. The NYSE requires larger numbers in each category. (If you'd like to see the exact listing requirements, visit www.nyse.com or www.nasdaq.com.)

But neither the NYSE nor the NASDAQ "bless" the issue in terms of its value or investment worth. They are merely listing companies that have stock that is traded. While the exchanges have requirements to keep the stocks listed, such as the amount of profit or number of shareholders, they are minimal at best. Don't look to the exchange or the NASDAQ to give you a level of comfort for investing. They're only mechanisms to facilitate the trading of stocks, nothing more.

The larger companies usually list on the NYSE, but some of the best known names such as Microsoft and Intel (which as of this writing are part of the Dow Jones Industrial Average of 30 stocks) are still on the NASDAQ. Traditionally, high-tech companies have started and stayed with NAS-DAQ. With the exceptions of technology and biotechnology, most of the larger companies are listed on the NYSE.

Some investors think that buying an NYSE stock will give a measure of safety because of the requirements for being traded on the exchange. You've just read why that isn't the case. Some very big names have been listed that are no longer with us. Enron pops to mind.

So there is no extra safety in being listed on the NYSE. There is also no extra safety just because a company is large. As of this writing, Merck is having major problems because of its drug Vioxx. There were several deaths of patients taking the drug—and although only a few suits have come to trial as of this writing, the stock has been hammered. Phillip Morris, which is part of Altria, has had litigation from cancer patients for years. Pfizer has recently had problems that sent its stock falling. GM, at this writing, is losing market share to the Japanese and had its debt downgraded to "junk" status from investment grade. That sent its common stock down noticeably until Kirk Kerkorian made an offer to buy millions of shares for $31 apiece. The stock then rallied to that price, but without that bid, the stock was hovering around $26 a share and looked to be headed lower.

Those are only a few examples of very large stocks with large problems. By the time you read this, there will be others that have suffered setbacks because of problems with their products or dishonesty of management or tough economic times. The point here is that no company is immune from human foibles (after all, humans are running them) or faulty products or tough economic times. Don't think a large company is a safe company. Although it may have the largest market share and suffer the least of its industry group when there are difficult times, it will be hurt just like any other stock. Never buy a company just because it's big. That's not enough of a reason. Big does not put you in your Comfort Zone.

PART TWO
DEFINITIONS

4

What's a Fed Head? The Big Picture and How to See It

If I say something and you understand it,
I've probably stated it incorrectly.

*—Attributed to Alan Greenspan, while
Chairman of the Federal Reserve System*

D on't skip this chapter. If we stay with our swimming analogy, it's the chapter that puts your head in the water. Some of you will have no problem; others will find it challenging. Either way, you have to get through it if you're going to swim in the deep end without stress. Once you understand this chapter, you'll be much closer to your Comfort Zone for investing.

We'll examine the Federal Reserve System (the Fed), interest rates, and major economic news releases, things that usually don't elicit great excitement in most readers, though you may be the exception. You have to know these things to get to your Comfort Zone.

The Fed is the strongest influence on the stock market. Extreme events have a temporary impact, but nothing has the lasting power of the Fed. We'll look at what the Fed is and does to warrant that power. This chapter also highlights the most closely watched economic announcements such as Leading Economic Indicators, the Consumer Price Index (CPI) and the Producer Price Index (PPI), and other noteworthy items that can gyrate markets.

I'll explain what the Fed is, how it works, and why it's important to your wealth. You'll also learn how powerful interest rates are and how to use them to your advantage. Knowing about the Fed and what its announcements mean will get you to your Comfort Zone much quicker than almost anything else.

More Than You Want to Know, but Exactly What You Have to Know

The Federal Reserve System

First, that's what the "Fed" is: the Federal Reserve System. You've most likely heard of its former chairman, Alan Greenspan, or its current chairman, Ben Bernanke. The chairman's the ultimate Fed Head, but there are other Fed Heads known as Fed governors. Some people believe the Fed chairman is the most powerful man in the world. Here's why.

The Federal Reserve System is the central bank of the United States, set up in 1913 by Congress to provide the nation with a safer, more flexible, more stable monetary and financial system. Its role has expanded considerably since its beginning.

Before Congress created the Fed, there were periodic financial panics that caused banks to collapse, business bankruptcies, and general economic downturns. In 1907 a particularly bad panic prompted Congress to establish the National Monetary Commission. Its purpose was to create an institution that would counter financial disruptions. On December 23, 1913, President Woodrow Wilson signed into law the Federal Reserve Act, which Congress had proposed.

The act's purpose: "To provide for the establishment of Federal reserve banks, to furnish an elastic currency, to afford means of rediscounting commercial paper, to establish a more effective supervision of banking in the United States, and for other purposes."

Over time, the Fed's purpose was clarified through acts such as the Banking Act of 1935, the Employment Act of 1946, the 1970 amendments to the Bank Holding Company Act, the International Banking Act of 1978, and several others. Congress defined the primary objectives of national economic policy in two acts: the Employment Act of 1946 and the Full Employment and Balanced Growth Act of 1978 (known as the Humphrey-Hawkins Act). The Fed's objectives now include economic growth in line with the economy's potential to expand, a high level of employment, stable prices (meaning stability in the purchasing power of the dollar), and moderate long-term interest rates.

To summarize, the Fed is supposed to help the economy grow, keep employment full, stabilize prices relative to the purchasing price of the dollar, and keep long-term interest rates from getting too high. That's a big job, and the irony is that the Fed doesn't have all the tools to deal with these challenges, especially as it pertains to interest rates.

For the most part, the Fed can move short-term interest rates up or down. However, it has a hard time influencing long-term rates, one of its mandates. That's because the Fed doesn't have a way of affecting the long-term rates. While it can actually move a short-term rate such as the Federal Funds rate (that's the rate banks charge to lend money to another bank—it's the most basic cost of money and usually is only done overnight to satisfy regulatory requirements), the Fed can't directly alter longer term rates except by something called a coupon pass. That's when the Fed sells Treasury bonds, thereby putting bonds in the market, which takes money out of the economy, or it buys Treasury bonds, adding money to the economy. That's a very short-term fix and doesn't change interest rates in a meaningful way.

Let's not get too deep here. I can sense your eyes are starting to glaze over. The point is that the Fed is required to do some things it can't. That doesn't mean it doesn't try. A little later in the chapter I'll explain how they do their best to comply with their mandate.

The Most Important Thing About the Fed

What really matters here is that when the Fed does change short-term interest rates, the stock market pays attention, particularly when the *direction* of interest rates changes. That usually signals a new cycle in the economy. If you gain nothing else except the awareness that the direction of interest rates is the most powerful factor on the stock market, you will have reached a new level of understanding about stocks.

When interest rates are going up, it means the economy is expanding. It can also mean that prices are going higher. Higher prices mean inflation. Inflation is simply this: The price of something is going up without that something changing. In other words, a gallon of gas that cost 25 cents in 1960 is the same gallon of gas that now costs $3.50. That's inflation. Or the house that cost $50,000 in 1975 and now costs $1,000,000 is a victim of inflation. But the long-distance phone call that costs 3 cents a minute and used to cost $1 is the result of productivity, brought about by new technology. Productivity is the antidote to inflation. The higher the productivity, the less likely it is inflation will occur.

The Fed is ever vigilant against inflation and wants to stop it before it gets out of control, the way it did in the '70s, when the government was trying to finance a war in Vietnam as well as many domestic programs. That era was referred to as "guns and butter" because the government was trying to pay for guns for the war and give "butter" in the form of aid to thousands of domestic programs. But economic reality doesn't allow taxes to pay for everything. Without enough tax revenues, the government had to borrow more money and print more of it to pay for social and military programs.

The ultimate cost of this hyper spending came in the form of extremely high interest rates that shut down the economy. The Fed had to stop the frenzy that was pushing prices higher and higher. Everyone believed that buying today was smart because most everything cost more the longer one waited for it. That psychology had to be broken. And it was the Fed, and particularly then-Chairman Paul Volcker, that had the strength to stop the escalating prices. Only after years of raising interest rates, which caused stock prices to crack and real estate values to fall, did American consumers and the government stop spending exuberantly.

The Fed doesn't want to have to step in to bring superhigh inflation down again. That's why preventing inflation is its number one priority. The Fed doesn't like raising interest rates to dizzying heights to stop spending and spiraling prices. It's no fun to be the villain, the guy who stops the party.

The strategy for the Fed is to be ahead of inflation, to try to slow the economy before things get out of hand. As this is written the Fed has been raising interest rates a modest amount every six weeks, trying to slow spending and prices. The economy doesn't show robust growth, but the Fed has announced it wants to move in a "measured" way, meaning slowly but surely until it sees that inflation won't be a problem.

That's what happens when the economy is growing nicely: no or low inflation. But there's a problem if the economy is growing too slowly, especially if the Fed has tightened interest rates to such a level that most business expansion stops. Then people get laid off. Remember, the Fed is supposed to help keep employment healthy.

In order to stimulate growth and keep employment strong, the Fed lowers interest rates. Broadly, that makes borrowing cheaper so people can buy more homes and cars and refrigerators. Again broadly, when those orders are placed, companies need to hire more workers to make those products. But if the Fed has to slow the economy by tightening rates, and it goes too far, unemployment rises, contrary to its mandate.

The Fed walks a very tight line. It needs to monitor all economic data to determine if things are heating up or slowing down. It has to act in the best interest of the economy in the long run, not the short run. That sometimes means taking unpopular stances and moving interest rates higher than most business people or politicians would like.

The Fed is an independent body, reporting to no one, at least in theory. That was one of the main objectives of the original act. Its creators wanted to be sure the Fed chairman and governors would act independently, without worrying about being voted out of office or reporting to someone who could be voted out. The Fed chairman is appointed by the president to serve for fourteen years. That way, he or she can take the long-term view when making decisions. Though appointed by the president, he or she is not supposed to be indebted or beholden to the president. However, the

Fed chairman must report to Congress at least once a year on the state of the economy. This usually is in the summer. The Fed chairman is now Ben Bernanke, who in 2006 replaced Alan Greenspan, who in 1987 replaced Paul Volcker.

The Famous FOMC

The Federal Open Market Committee (the FOMC) is the governing body of the Federal Reserve System. It has 12 members: 7 members of the Board of Governors of the Fed, the president of the Federal Reserve Bank of New York, and 4 members from the other 11 Federal Reserve Banks who serve for one-year terms. They meet eight times a year to determine policies that will achieve long-term price stability and sustainable economic growth. These are the meetings you want to monitor, but not too intensely.

You don't have to work hard to know what happened at these meetings. CNBC and other networks have a journalist outside the Fed building after every meeting to report on what the Fed decided. Whether they raise interest rates, lower them, do nothing, or establish new policies, it is reported on television and in the newspapers that day. These are often market-moving announcements, especially when there's a surprise.

Every Fed meeting is scheduled well in advance. Go to the Online Investor (www.theonlineinvestor.com) and look in the Market Calendar section for the dates. You can also use the Fed site: www.federalreserve.gov/FOMC/. When the Fed meets, investors watch with great anticipation, because if the Fed moves interest rates significantly higher or lower, it sends a signal that things are worse than anticipated.

Before each Fed meeting, economists speculate as to what the Fed will do. You can read their ideas in most newspapers or watch them debate on CNBC or Bloomberg TV or other business channels. What these economists predict has no influence on the Fed, but it does tell investors what most experts are expecting. That's what the stock market is priced for: the consensus expectations of the experts.

Let's say the experts (and they're sometimes wrong because they don't have the extensive data that the Fed uses to make their decisions) are looking for the Fed to raise interest rates by 25 basis points. That's equal to

¼ of 1 percent of a point or .25%. That's the normal amount the Fed moves rates, up or down, unless it wants to slow down or speed up the economy more quickly. Then it will move 50 basis points or .50% of a point. In extreme cases it will move the rates by 75 basis points, but that is very rare.

This is why you need to follow and understand the Fed. It can move the stock and bond markets, sometimes in a big way. And interest rates are its moving tools. I'll explain how interest rates affect the markets in a little while, but right now just focus on a few more facts about the Fed.

It meets eight times a year, and after each meeting, announces whether it will change interest rates. Economists will make their best guesses as to what that announcement will be, even if it is that there will be no change in rates. The Fed is always trying to keep the economy moving forward, to keep employment full, and to keep the dollar's purchasing power stable. Smart investors watch the Fed closely and understand that stocks will react when it changes policies regarding interest rates.

Party Time!

Think of the Fed this way: Imagine the economy as a big party with everyone invited. The Fed is the catering service, wearing black tuxedoes, serving drinks. It brings out the punch bowls at the beginning of the party (that's when it lowers interest rates). Everyone starts drinking and mingling. As the guests drink more, the party heats up and starts to look like it might get out of hand (this is equivalent to inflation showing up in the economy). The Fed, as the responsible caterer, removes several of the punch bowls (which is when they raise interest rates). Now there are fewer bowls (i.e., there is less money and it's more costly because of higher interest rates). People need to look harder for them and take less from them, but they're still drinking. If they're still getting out of hand, the Fed takes away more bowls (raises interest rates again).

When enough bowls have been removed, people start to quiet down, dancing becomes less exuberant, some guests get very sick (go bankrupt). The Fed is very happy. Except now, because it is responsible for keeping the party going, it worries that it took away too many punch bowls (raised interest rates too high). So just when it looks like people are going to start fighting over the little bit of punch left or are heading to the couches to snooze for a while (higher unemployment), the Fed grabs some punch bowls and puts them back on the table (lowers interest rates).

The party can't stop. The Fed has to keep it going. If only a few punch bowls doesn't draw enough people back in, the Fed puts out more bowls (lowers rates even more), until finally the mild roar that signals a happy group is heard once again. If that mild roar gets too loud, some of the punch bowls get taken away again. And so the party goes.

Here's the catch for the Fed: It can take away punch bowls (raise interest rates) and the party will definitely slow. But when the party dies down and more punch is served (interest rates are lowered), it can't make guests drink (borrow money). That's the ultimate irony for the Fed. It can stop the economy from overheating, but it can't make it get up and go. But thanks to human nature and its needs, the economy always does.

When the Fed is lowering interest rates and nothing happens, it can continue to lower them. Until they reach a level at which people will spend and reactivate the economy, the lower rates don't help. To throw in another metaphor, it's like pushing on a string. It doesn't do anything. So as powerful as the Fed is, it can't make people or companies spend money.

The concern is very real when the economy is sluggish and the psychology is negative. Fear rules investors and the consumer. They're afraid things will get worse and worse, and that the only way to survive is to hang on to their money. By doing so, they only slow the economy more.

Become a Fed Head

Watch the Fed. Read more about it. Check out its Web site (www.federal reserve.gov). Understand it at a very basic level: It's the watchdog of the economic party. When it's raising interest rates, the stock market usually has a harder time going up. When it's lowering rates, the stock market usually does better. (I use "usually" because nothing is absolute in the stock market. I'll go into some scenarios a little later that explain why sometimes, the opposite of what you expect happens.) Follow the Fed meetings. Remember, when the Fed *changes the direction* of interest rates, it is meaningful to the market.

Understanding Interest Rates and How They Move Markets

From the above description, you can tell interest rates are powerful tools. The Fed uses them to accomplish its goals as best it can. Here's how interest rates work.

Interest rates tell you the cost of money. The higher they are, the more money costs. Like everything else, if something goes too high in price, people don't buy it. If rates are very low, lots of people buy and use money.

The most basic interest rate is the Federal Funds rate. It's the rate banks charge each other for borrowing money, usually overnight. The Fed funds rate is where interest rates start. From that rate, other rates are determined. For example, if the Fed funds rate is 1% (for overnight money), then money borrowed for a week will cost more, just as money for a month, a year, five years, or longer would cost more. If you plot interest rates on a graph, that graph is called a yield curve. It shows you what money costs at any one point in time, from overnight borrowing to 30 years. Normally, it shows lower rates for the short end of the curve and higher rates as the number of years increases. That's called the "normal" yield curve. Again, at the very beginning of the curve is the Fed funds rate. It's the one that all the other rates are based on.

If the Fed is raising the Fed funds rate, then the cost of borrowing usually goes up all along the yield curve. Car loans cost more. Rates for new mortgages and many adjustable mortgages go up. All borrowings cost more the day after the Fed raises Fed funds in a normal economic environment.

Why Interest Rates Matter to Stocks

With that thought in mind, let's look at how stocks are affected by interest rates. To do that you need to know the theory behind stock pricing. Did you ever wonder how a stock gets to the price it is? What is shaping that price at this particular time?

Two of the most powerful influencers on stock prices are the future earnings of the stock and interest rates. That's because the theoretical current price of a stock is the discounted future value of all its earnings and dividends. That means that if a stock is expected to earn $1 this year, then $1.10 next year, $1.20 the next, and so on for 10 years or more, then the stock is worth all of those years of earnings. Except that you can't just add those earnings up and get the price because those earnings are coming in the future.

That means two things: Those earnings are not certain, and they are not worth as much today since they won't be made until years from now. There are two elements in the stock price: How certain are the earnings that are projected, and how much are they worth today?

Earnings are always uncertain. That's where the term "risk premium" plays into the stock price. The more certain the earnings are, the lower the risk premium. The more uncertainty, the higher the risk premium is (meaning the lower the stock price and the more volatile its price).

As for the second element, the worth or value of those earnings today is easier to calculate because that value is a factor of interest rates. Earlier, I mentioned the term "discounted future value." It means that you discount the future earnings back to the present to get their value, then add those up to get the price. (In reality, you as the individual investor won't be doing this, but you need to understand this part of stock pricing if you're going to have a concept of value for stocks.)

Here's how discounting future earnings works. If you are looking at $1 of earnings in one year, what is that $1 worth today? It's not worth $1 because if I had a dollar, I could put it in a Treasury bill and earn interest on it so it would be worth $1.03 in a year as of this writing. (That's just by buying a Treasury bill that yields 3% now and in a year receiving my principal and interest of 3%.) So if I hold on to that $1 in one year it is worth less than $1 today. In this interest-rate environment, it's worth 3% less, if the earnings are absolutely assured. Again, the risk premium comes into play here. If those earnings are highly suspect, then 3% is not the right "discount rate" because that rate is the lowest level of risk, the U.S. Treasury. Buying stock is like lending that $1 to a distant cousin who's just gotten out of jail versus lending it to your brother who is a banker. You'd charge different rates to each because the likelihood of getting it back depends on who borrows it.

So that future $1 isn't worth $1 today. It's worth less, exactly 2.9 cents less. That assumes a 3% Treasury bill rate. With this example it's worth about 97.1 cents. (It's not 97 because the return of 3 cents on an investment of 97 cents is 3.09%, which is 3 divided by 97.) There are math tables that give you the discount rate for any level. The point here is that $1 in a year (the discounted future value) is worth 97.1 cents when the 1-year Treasury rate is 3%.

If you add a "risk premium" to that future $1, then it will be worth less than 97.1 cents. And all the future dollars will have to be discounted according to the interest rate that applies for that time frame. For example, if the company is expected to grow earnings and 5 years from now is anticipated to make $1.50, then you would take the 5-year interest rate and discount that $1.50 back to today. In this example, assume that the rate is 5% for the 5 years. And each year going out is higher. As you do the math, you see the farther out in years you go, the less valuable that $1 is in today's terms. After about 10 years, with the uncertainty of earnings and the high discount rates used, that future $1 becomes useless in a calculation.

Get This Part

Here's where the power of interest rates comes in. If interest rates go up, then the future value of those earnings goes down. Let me repeat that because it's the very essence of why interest rates matter: If interest rates go up, the future value of earnings goes down. That means the stock price goes down. If the Fed raises rates in this example to let's say 4%, then that future $1 in one year is worth only 96.15 cents today, almost a penny less. Doesn't sound like much, but it is.

That's because the whole yield curve will have shifted upward, and each future dollar becomes less valuable. So when you add up the current value of those future earnings, it's much less than when rates were starting at 3%. And that's why interest rates are so powerful: They change the value of future earnings and therefore the price of a stock. Of course, higher interest rates also increase the uncertainty of those future earnings because the economy will most likely be slowing due to the higher rates. Analysts have to lower their earning estimates because of that uncertainty. So future earnings are lowered, then they're discounted to a lower value because of the higher rates used in the math. As you can see, higher rates carry a double whammy.

If you're still with me, you can see why raising interest rates can have such a powerful impact on stock investors. Higher rates make future earnings less valuable today, AND they increase the uncertainty of expectations of what earnings will be.

On the other side of the interest-rate coin is what happens when rates are lowered. Then the reverse happens. Future earnings become more valuable because the "discount" rate used is lowered. That makes those earnings worth more today. While the expectations may be more certain, it's not guaranteed because lower rates usually mean the economy is slowing. That can make future earnings less predictable as well.

In summary, interest rates matter to stock investors. When they go up, stock prices go down because future earnings are worth less. When rates go down, future earnings are worth more. That's why you have to be aware of interest rates and the direction they're going. Keep up on interest rates. They'll give you a good indicator of the direction the stock market will most likely take.

Watch for These 9 Economic Indicators

There are many announcements made by the Fed and other government bodies that will help you make good guesses about the direction interest rates will go. Here are the most important ones to follow.

The Unemployment Report

It comes out the first Friday of every month. The higher employment goes, the more likely the Fed will raise interest rates. (The exception is when unemployment has been very high and people are starting to go back to work. Then the employment figure will rise but the Fed won't do anything.) It's only when unemployment starts to go below 6% that the Fed usually starts worrying about employment figures. This is because when many people are working, more wages are being paid, which in turn means more people will want more goods and services. When too many people are trying to buy the same products or services, then the price of those items goes up, thereby causing inflation.

Remember inflation is the number one enemy as far as the Fed is concerned. Watch this report. It's issued by the Labor Department and is released at 8:30 A.M. EST. It's carried live on CNBC and other business channels. You can read the details on most of the economic Web sites such as Yahoo!Finance, MSN, AOL Personal Finance, etc. Again, it's meaningful when employment rates are very high (above 8%) or very low (below 4%). These levels usually require the Fed to act by raising rates when employment is very high or lowering rates when it's too low.

Monthly Retail Sales

This comes out near the middle of the month, reporting sales of the last month. Since consumers represent about 67% of economic activity in the United States, these sales are closely watched. If the economy is to grow, consumers have to keep spending and not just on items they have to buy like groceries and drugs. The two gorillas in retail sales to watch are Wal-Mart and Target. They're so well implanted around the country that they give a good idea of how the average consumer is spending. Watch for the reported numbers as well as the forecasted ones. It's the expectations that most investors react to. If either or both have good announcements for the past month but warn of slowing sales for the next one, the market will most likely go down because investors believe that if these two retailers are seeing slower sales ahead, then most other pockets of the economy will as well.

Gross Domestic Product

Referred to as GDP, this measures the strength or weakness of the American economy. It's the sum of all business activity. If it's in a growth range of 3% to 4%, on an annual basis, that's solid improvement with little likelihood of inflation. There are three announcements for each quarter. The first is the initial reading. The second is the revised reading, and almost every quarter is revised a little down or up. The third is the final and official number, which may or may not be different from the revised number, but if so it is usually not in a meaningful way. If the GDP grows less than 3%, the fear is that economic activity is slowing and maybe unemployment will rise. That's bad for the market. If the GDP is increasing by more than 4%, the fear is that inflation will come back and prices will rise. That's also bad for the market. See how hard the Fed's job is—since it's supposed to keep the economy growing without inflation and to keep employment high?

Monthly Auto Sales

These are announced at the beginning of each month, usually on the first or second business day. Because auto sales are one of the engines of the economy (autos require a lot of workers, heavy investment in equipment, financing to buy them, etc.), these are watched closely. If they slow too much, it can be an indicator of economic sluggishness just around the next curve. Also, if the Fed is raising interest rates, these sales will be affected because the monthly payments for credit buyers will be higher and exclude some buyers. If rates are going down, sales should increase because more buyers can qualify for cars.

Monthly New Home Sales

New homes are monitored much like cars because they require so many resources to build. From the lumber to the carpets to the appliances, new homes demand goods and services from many sectors of the economy. When new home sales are going strong, it's a good indicator of economic health. Because almost all new homes are bought with a mortgage, this sector is sensitive to interest rates. When the Fed is tightening rates, fewer new homes are bought because monthly payments are higher, thus eliminating many new, first-time buyers. The exception is when the Fed is tightening rates (remember they can only effectively tighten the short rates), but longer interest rates don't go up. This happens when investors believe the Fed's current moves will prevent inflation and that future interest rates will not be going higher. In that case, which is what is happening as I write this, fixed rate mortgages, which are tied mostly to the 10-year treasury rate, will not go up. When this happens, even though the Fed is tightening, new home sales continue to do well because the cost of money (the interest rate to borrow it) is not going up. New home sales are a good indicator of the health of the economy. They're closely watched by the pros.

The CPI and PPI

These stand for Consumer Price Index and Producer Price Index. The CPI measures the cost of goods that consumers pay. In other words, when you and I buy a shirt or a gallon of gas or anything else, we pay the consumer price.

The PPI is what the companies that make the stuff pay for goods that you and I buy. In other words, they buy it wholesale, add value to the product (think of buying cotton and sewing it into a shirt), then sell it to us.

The CPI is an inflation gauge. If it is going higher, it means prices are moving up. Without similar gains in productivity, this will cause inflation. The PPI may also foretell inflation except when the manufacturers can't pass along their rising costs in the form of higher prices. In other words, it may cost the manufacturer more to buy raw materials but it may not be able to raise its prices to the customer to recover the increased cost. That's because of competition.

Competition is a wonderful thing if you're a consumer. It guarantees you can buy things at their lowest prices. If one manufacturer can make a pair of jeans at a lower cost, it can sell those jeans at a lower price than its competitors. The same is true for cars, beds, anything that is made with labor and materials. If the PPI shows price increases, it doesn't necessarily mean consumers will be paying more for goods. That's because many competitive goods are made in foreign countries with lower costs for labor and/or materials. Since they are making their products without the higher costs that domestic manufacturers have, they can price their goods according to their price structure, not the U.S. price structure.

Think of a car manufacturer in South Korea competing with General Motors. The higher costs of U. S. steel and labor don't affect the South Korean company. It can price its cars based on its cost structure, not the U.S. cost structure. That means its cars will be less expensive. The debate comes in as to whether they are built as well, but that argument goes away since many consumers judge quality with their pocketbooks.

What a rising PPI will do to manufacturers is squeeze profit margins unless prices to the consumer can be raised. Squeezed profit margins mean lower earnings per share. That will translate into lower stock prices.

That's why you have to look at both the CPI and the PPI to see what they mean for your stocks, especially if you own manufacturing stocks. A rising PPI without an increase in the CPI means less profits, and if that continues over a few months, it will show up in lower earnings. Also, any sharp spike in either of these indexes will not be well received by investors since it suggests prices have moved up and may continue in that direction, sounding the bell for inflation. These two indexes can move the market strongly if they report much higher than expected numbers.

Consumer Sentiment

This is published once a month and gives a reading on how consumers are feeling about the economy. It's compiled by the University of Michigan and tries to measure how consumers will act in the foreseeable future. If its polling shows optimism about jobs and the economy, the inference is that consumers will be more likely to spend. If it shows consumers are feeling depressed or negative about the future, they're less likely to spend.

This report is watched closely but doesn't have as much sway as others because it only shows how a participant felt at the time of the survey. It doesn't record actual spending habits. If it moves in a meaningful way in one month, it can be a factor for the stock market, at least on the day it's announced.

Leading Economic Indicators

This survey is intended to predict future economic activity. Typically, three consecutive monthly LEI changes in the same direction suggest a turning point in the economy. For example, three consecutive negative readings would indicate a possible recession. It's reported monthly by the Conference Board, a nonprofit group of business leaders.

The index of leading economic indicators (LEI) is a composite of 11 leading indicators: Average workweek (manufacturing); Initial unemployment claims; New orders for consumer goods; Vendor performance; Plant and equipment orders; Building permits; Change in unfilled durable orders; Sensitive material prices; Stock prices (S&P 500); Real M2 (a measure of the money supply); Index of consumer expectations.

Because the data presented in this index has a time lag of four to five weeks, it isn't a powerful influence on the stock or bond markets. In other words, most of the individual datum has already been announced. It is used as a forecasting tool to estimate future growth in the economy. If there is a strong move up or down in this index, it will have a short-term affect on the market.

Jobless Claims

This is issued by the U.S. Labor Department on a monthly basis. If jobless claims are going up, it means more people are unemployed, suggesting the economy is weakening. That means lower prices for stocks since layoffs would reduce the buying power of the workers who are out of jobs. Less buying power means less spending, which means lower sales for manufacturers of goods and services.

If claims are down, it means more people are working and suggests better economic activity. When the economy is starting to recover, this announcement is watched closely as an early indicator of better times ahead. If the economy is already moving along at a nice pace, the claims number is less important.

There are other releases that grab the headlines from time to time, but the above reports carry the most weight as of this writing. By understanding what they represent, you can stay in your Comfort Zone when the news hits the fan. You don't have to follow all the forecasts and stay glued to your television for the actual announcements. You'll see them on the evening news or on your favorite financial Web site or in the newspapers. There will be other indicators that come to the attention of forecasters. At one time the money supply was followed obsessively every week. Then that faded, and other factors emerged as having the most "meaning," as far as the pundits were concerned.

These are the current "hot" buttons. Others will take their place. The key to helping you to stay in your Comfort Zone is to know what these announcements mean and why they are moving the stock market. One helpful place to find an explanation of any of the economic releases is the Web site Ask (www.ask.com). This site finds other Web sites that will answer most of your questions. You just have to remember to put your inquiry in the form of a question to get the best results. For example, if you wanted to know what the Leading Economic Indicators were, you would type in "What are the Leading Economic Indicators?" and it would find the sites with explanations of the term.

Take a moment to reread the above economic reports. The next time you hear that the PPI jumped, you'll know what that means. You'll think to look up what the CPI has been doing (use Ask or another search engine to find it), and see what the trends are for both of these indexes. If the PPI is going up but the CPI is staying flat, you'll know that profit margins are being squeezed at companies. If you own stock in manufacturers, you will want to look at them as possible sale candidates, then dig into their latest earnings reports and determine how they're coping with this squeeze on profits. (I'll tell you how to do this in a later chapter.) If their profitability is waning, and you believe the trend will continue, it will be an easy decision to sell those stocks.

This is what Comfort Zone investing is all about: taking the stress out of buying and selling stocks through understanding events that affect the capital markets. While no one number is a conclusive trigger that makes you buy or sell, each of the data points of a stock or the stock market gives you a better understanding of the "Big Picture" of investing. The more you get the picture, both large and small, the more comfortable you'll be with your decisions.

Don't Do Anything Based on One Number

The one thing you don't want to do is buy or sell a stock or bond based on one number. In the above example about the PPI, you wouldn't sell anything based on the report of a higher number. You'd be jumping in and out of stocks all the time if you made decisions based on the latest news. The idea is to make a rational decision based on many factors and *not* make quick ones based on a headline.

Think through whatever news is making the market move. If you own drug stocks, they're not going to be affected by the PPI or the latest Fed announcement on interest rates. The drug companies make a product that is immune to most economic influences because they make a product that people need no matter what else is happening in the economy. That's why drug stocks are called defensive investments.

That doesn't mean they only go up in value. As mentioned earlier, at this writing Pfizer and Merck are battling issues concerning Viagra and Vioxx, respectively. Each industry has its weak spots. Some of them have to do with the health of the general economy, such as autos, homes, and banks, which are sensitive to interest rates. Others are moved by product safety, such as drugs. This is a big part of being in your Comfort Zone: knowing what news moves your stocks. In the next chapter, I'll go over industries and sectors, giving you insight into the characteristics of the major ones and what events influence them.

What's Happening Now, Economically Speaking

One of the basic elements of investing is to know whether the economy is expanding or contracting. Certain investments will act better when it's expanding and others will be more rewarding when it's contracting.

The signs that the economy is expanding are more people are employed (see the Employment Report); interest rates are going higher (see the latest Fed announcements); retail sales are increasing (see the Retail Sales releases); auto sales are better (see the Auto Sales news); new home sales are picking up (see the New Homes Sales report). When you see all of these going in a positive direction, you can be certain the economy is improving (also described as expanding).

That means you'll want to own stocks that will benefit from this expansion. Some examples would be auto supply firms, furniture manufacturers, plumbing manufacturers, auto makers, new home builders, steel producers.

Most companies benefit from an expanding economy, especially in the early stages of the expansion.

What puts a wrench in the gears for gauging the expansion is the interest-rate factor. As already mentioned, the direction of interest rates will tell you what is happening in the economy. If the Fed is raising interest rates because it perceives the economy is expanding or about to expand too quickly, it won't stop the recovery if its increases in rates are small, such as ¼ of 1 percent or 25 basis points, unless it does so over an extended period of time. It's only when the Fed takes dramatic action, such as moving rates 50 basis points or ½ of 1 percent, that the stock market will get spooked. Taking a "measured" approach to raising interest rates will not slow an expanding economy nor will it stop the stock market from improving.

The exception is when the economy is booming, and the Fed has real concerns about inflation roaring back. Then it will make major moves in interest rates to slow things down. When the Fed is moving interest rates higher in large chunks, the stock market will definitely move down.

When the economy is contracting or slowing too much, the Fed will lower interest rates. The market almost always likes lower rates. Again, the direction is important here. If the Fed begins to lower rates after a prolonged period of raising rates or keeping them flat, it signals a weakening of the economy. If the Fed moves them down dramatically, the market won't like that because it suggests the economy is in really bad shape. Once again, if the Fed moves in a measured way, lowering rates by only 25 basis points, it signals there is some concern that the economy is slowing and that a little help from the Fed is needed. That will usually be well received by the markets because lower rates will mean more borrowing power for corporations and individuals, which will translate into more spending and a healthier economy.

You, as an investor, have almost as difficult a task as the Fed. You want to invest in stocks that will flourish with an expanding economy but not be overweighted in them if the economy begins to contract. Conversely, you want to be in mostly defensive stocks when the economy is contracting. It seems like a mission impossible, one that doesn't allow for a Comfort Zone. But you can have a Comfort Zone in all types of economic directions. I'll show you how in chapter 6 that describes the Core Portfolio.

The Fed and Alice

The final thought about interest rates and the Fed is to understand that they—and we—can live in Alice's wonderland world at times. Good can mean bad and bad can mean good. Here's what I mean.

When the economy is very weak but starting to improve, jobless claims go down as people find jobs. That's good. That means more people are being employed. But when the economy already has full employment (when unemployment is below 5%), and jobless claims go down, that's bad because more people are employed, which means even more spending. With more spending in a strong economy, there is a good chance of inflation. With more inflation, the Fed will step in to slow down the economy. So jobless claims going down isn't always a good thing, only when the economy is slow.

Another example: When rates are very low from a slow economy, and the Fed lowers them again, that's a bad sign. It means the Fed isn't seeing economic activity strong enough to warrant a halt to lowering rates, much less raising them. Investors interpret this action as bad for stocks because earnings will mostly likely continue to be weak from the slow economy.

Conversely, in a strong economy, after the Fed has been raising for several quarters or years, and the Fed lowers rates, that's a good sign. That means the economic activity is slowing enough so that the Fed is worried that further expansion is in jeopardy. If the economy doesn't respond to the first round of cuts by showing increased employment, lower prices, etc., the Fed will lower rates again, which in turn will give investors reasons to be positive on future growth and higher profits.

The key here is that you have to be aware of economic extremes. That's when good news becomes bad and bad news can be good. The data released, in and of itself, doesn't tell you enough about how the markets will react. You have to stay aware of where the economy is in its cycle. One easy way to do that is to monitor the employment rate. When the unemployment rate is very low, close to 5% or below, the economy is doing very well. When the unemployment gets close to 7%, the economy is doing poorly. Those aren't the only numbers to follow, but they will give a good indication of the overall health of the economy.

Again, understand the elements of this chapter, and you won't be surprised by the next Fed announcement, the latest news releases from the Labor Department, or any other economic releases. Also, it's rare that any of these will trigger a buy or sell decision for your stocks. These data should be seen as indicators of what is happening in the economy, and it's the trend over several announcements that will help you determine the state of the economy. Remember, the more you understand, the deeper you'll get into your Comfort Zone.

5

Sectors and Industry Groups

I don't like money actually, but it quiets my nerves.

—*Joe Louis, boxer*

I mentioned earlier that you must know what you own. If you don't, you have no idea of when to buy or sell. This chapter is about putting your stocks into categories so you can achieve a balance in your investments. As in life, being balanced in your portfolio is part of being in your Comfort Zone. To achieve that balance, you have to understand Sectors and Industries.

What's a Sector?

Sectors are broad categories that include several industry groups. The list isn't very long: Basic Materials, Conglomerates, Consumer Goods, Financial, Health Care, Industrial Goods, Services, Technology, and Utilities.

The reason you want to understand sectors is that your portfolio should never be invested in only one sector. To reach a balance, you need to have at least three or four sectors represented. That's because each sector will react differently to changes in the economy and/or to interest rates.

For example, if you held stocks like Bank of America, American Express, Washington Mutual, Citigroup, Met Life, and Arden Realty, you would have various industries: banks, credit cards, insurance companies, and property management. But they would all be in the same sector—Financial. They would all generally move in the same direction when interest rates went up or down. When rates go up, this sector has traditionally gone down. When interest rates go down, the sector has usually gone up. So your whole portfolio will be moving in one direction with no counterbalancing stocks that move the opposite way if you hold only Financial sector stocks.

This concept is important and goes to the heart of Comfort Zone investing. You are looking to maximize your sense of well-being and do well in the stock market. You are not looking to maximize your investments. In order to only maximize your returns, you would have to take exceptional risks that would push you far from a Comfort Zone. In fact, when you try only to maximize your returns, you maximize your discomfort, the very antithesis of our goal in this book. And you may not be successful in achieving those big returns since, by definition, high-risk investing means large losses as well as gains. If too many losses come before the gains, you're out of the game.

The best way to stay in your Comfort Zone is to own enough stocks to be diversified. But those stocks must be in different sectors or you raise your risk level. The following sectors are listed with the Industry Groups under them. Use this to check your current stock holdings or to start a new balanced portfolio. Your goal is to own at least 10 to 12 stocks that are in 3 or 4 sectors. You'll find out more about which stocks to buy in the section on the Core Portfolio in chapter 6.

These Sectors and Industry Groups are taken from Yahoo!Finance (http://biz.yahoo.com). If you want to find specific companies (which are too numerous to list here), then go to the site and scroll down the page. On the left side, under the heading of Investing, click on the link for Industries. You'll find them arranged by Sectors. By clicking on the Industry under the Sector heading, you'll go to the stocks that make up the Industry Group.

Sector: Basic Materials

INDUSTRY GROUPS: Agricultural Chemicals, Aluminum, Chemicals—Major Diversified, Copper, Gold, Independent Oil and Gas, Industrial Metals and Minerals, Major Integrated Oil and Gas, Nonmetallic Mineral Mining, Oil and Gas Drilling Exploration, Oil and Gas Equipment and Services, Oil and Gas Pipelines, Oil and Gas Refining and Marketing, Silver, Specialty Chemicals, Steel and Iron, Synthetics.

COMMON CHARACTERISTICS: This group tends to be the first to experience economic events. If the economy is beginning to pick up, there are more orders for steel, chemicals, and aluminum as manufacturers begin to build more cars, homes, and appliances. When the economy is weakening, these groups are the first to see a slowdown in orders. Basic Materials are good to own when the economy is coming out of a recession or a slowdown in the economy. Conversely, if the economy is finishing a boom period, this group will swoon first and fast.

Sector: Conglomerates

INDUSTRY GROUPS: Conglomerates (such as GE, 3M, Tyco).

COMMON CHARACTERISTICS: These are large groups of companies under one heading. GE, for example, builds locomotive engines, has a financing arm, makes appliances and light bulbs and owns the NBC network. These are difficult companies to follow for stock analysts because they have such a diversity of revenue sources. This sector is almost always good to own because of that diversity. Instead of being focused in one area of the economy, the conglomerates usually have products in several of them. These stocks will often move with the economy and are best bought at the beginning of a recovery.

Sector: Consumer Goods

INDUSTRY GROUPS: Appliances, Auto Manufacturers—Major, Auto Parts, Beverages—Alcohol, Beverages—Soft Drinks, Beverages—Wineries and Distillers, Business Equipment, Cigarettes, Cleaning Products, Confectioners,

Dairy Products, Electronic Equipment, Farm Products, Food—Major Diversified, Home Furnishings and Fixtures, Housewares and Accessories, Meat Products, Office Supplies, Packaging and Containers, Paper and Paper Products, Personal Products, Photographic Equipment and Supplies, Processed and Packaged Goods, Recreational Goods, Recreational Vehicles, Rubber and Plastics, Sporting Goods, Textile—Apparel Clothing, Textile—Apparel Footwear and Accessories, Tobacco Products, Toys and Games, Trucks and Other Vehicles.

COMMON CHARACTERISTICS: There are very few commonalities among these industries except that they are all bought by the consumer. However, some of them like Dairy Products, Cleaning Products, Farm Products, and Meat Products are staples of most homes so they'll be bought most of the time, no matter what the economy is doing. Items such as Autos, Photo Equipment, and Recreational Goods and Vehicles are all discretionary goods that are sensitive to consumers' incomes, which go down when unemployment goes up. Therefore, as an investor, you need to look at each industry group and determine which ones are necessary and which ones are more in the "luxury" category. The more basic or necessary the goods, the less likely the manufacturers will be hurt by the economy. That also means less volatility in the stock price. The trade-off is that there is strong competition in the basic necessities, and the profit margins are always very thin. That means lower valuations for the stocks because the potential of strong upside surprises in earnings is not there.

Sector: Financial

INDUSTRY GROUPS: Accident and Health Insurance, Asset Management, Credit Services, Diversified Investments, Foreign Money Center Banks, Foreign Regional Banks, Insurance Brokers, Investment Brokerage—National, Investment Brokerage—Regional, Life Insurance, Money Center Banks, Mortgage Investment, Property and Casualty Insurance, REIT (Real Estate Investment Trust)—Diversified, REIT—Health Care Facilities, REIT—Hotel/Motel, REIT—Industrial, REIT—Office, REIT—Residential, REIT—Retail, Real Estate Development, Regional—Mid-Atlantic Banks,

Regional—Midwest Banks, Regional—Northeast Banks, Regional—Pacific Banks, Regional—Southeast Banks, Regional—Southwest Banks, Savings and Loans, Surety and Title Insurance.

COMMON CHARACTERISTICS: Very sensitive to interest rates. Though many of the banks and savings and loans make adjustable rate mortgages, which move up when interest rates increase, they are still viewed by investors as interest-rate sensitive, partly because there are fewer mortgages made when rates go higher. Fewer mortgages mean lower revenues from fees and interest payments. All of the stocks in the Financial sector benefit when interest rates go down. When the Fed starts decreasing interest rates, and early in a recovery, they are good to own. Conversely, when interest rates are rising and the economy is slowing, financial stocks don't do well.

Sector: Health Care

INDUSTRY GROUPS: Biotechnology, Diagnostic Substances, Drug Delivery, Drug Manufacturers—Major, Drug Manufacturers—Other, Drug-Related Products, Drugs—Generic, Health Care Plans, Home Health Care, Hospitals, Long-Term Care Facilities, Medical Appliances and Equipment, Medical Instruments and Supplies, Medical Laboratories and Research, Medical Practitioners, Specialized Health Services.

COMMON CHARACTERISTICS: Indifferent to interest rates. Most of these groups will benefit from the aging of the baby boomers. As they grow older, they need more and more medical services. Health Care stocks are good defensive investments that are not economically sensitive. These are stocks to own in good and bad times.

Sector: Industrial Goods

INDUSTRY GROUPS: Aerospace/Defense—Major Diversified, Aerospace/Defense Products and Services, Cement, Diversified Machinery, Farm and Construction Machinery, General Building Materials, General Contractors, Heavy Construction, Industrial Electrical Equipment, Industrial Equipment and Components, Lumber, Wood Production, Machine Tools and

Accessories, Manufactured Housing, Metal Fabrication, Pollution and Treatment Controls, Residential Construction, Small Tools and Accessories, Textile Industrial, Waste Management.

COMMON CHARACTERISTICS: Good to own at the beginning of an economic recovery. The industrial goods sector has companies that benefit from new construction of buildings, highways, airports, and airplanes, commercial or military. These stocks perform well at the beginning of and during an economic recovery but fall quickly when a slowdown begins or investors think one will begin.

Sector: Services

INDUSTRY GROUPS: Advertising Agencies, Air Delivery & Freight Services, Air Services—Other, Apparel Stores, Auto Dealerships, Auto Parts Stores, Auto Parts Wholesale, Basic Materials Wholesale, Broadcasting—Radio, Broadcasting—Television, Building Materials Wholesale, Business Services, CATV Systems, Catalog & Mail Order Houses, Computers Wholesale, Consumer Services, Department Stores, Discount, Variety Stores, Drug Stores, Drugs Wholesale, Education & Training Services, Electronics—Wholesale, Entertainment—Diversified, Food Wholesale, Gaming Activities, General Entertainment, Grocery Stores, Home Furnishing Stores, Home Improvement Stores, Industrial Equipment Wholesale, Jewelry Stores, Lodging, Major Airlines, Management Services, Marketing Services, Medical Equipment Wholesale, Movie Production & Theaters, Music and Video Stores, Personal Services, Publishing—Books, Publishing—Newspapers, Publishing—Periodicals, Railroads, Regional Airlines, Rental & Leasing Services, Research Services, Resorts & Casinos, Restaurants, Security & Protection Services, Shipping, Specialty Eateries, Specialty Retail—Other, Sporting Activities, Sporting Goods Stores, Staffing & Outsourcing Services, Technical Services, Toy & Hobby Stores, Trucking, Wholesale—Other.

COMMON CHARACTERISTICS: Not many. However, this group is labor intensive. When the economy is doing very well, employee costs rise as companies need to pay more to hire and retain good workers. When the economy is weaker and unemployment is high, these companies need fewer workers. If you own only stocks in this industry group, be aware that these companies see their assets leave the building every day. If the critical people don't return the following morning, the company is devastated.

Sector: Technology

INDUSTRIAL GROUPS: Application Software, Business Software & Services, Communication Equipment, Computer-Based Systems, Computer Peripherals, Data Storage Devices, Diversified Communication Services, Diversified Computer Systems, Diversified Electronics, Health Care Information Services, Information & Delivery Services, Information Technology Services, Internet Information Providers, Internet Service Providers, Internet Software & Services, Long-Distance Carriers, Multimedia & Graphics Software, Networking & Communication Devices, Personal Computers, Printed Circuit Boards, Processing Systems & Products, Scientific & Technical Instruments, Security Software & Services, Semiconductor—Broad Line, Semiconductor—Integrated Circuits, Semiconductor—Specialized, Semiconductor Equipments & Materials, Semiconductor—Memory Chips, Technical & System Software, Telecom Services—Domestic, Telecom Services—Foreign, Wireless Communications.

COMMON CHARACTERISTICS: High tech. Though there are many different types of companies in this sector, they all share the strong dependence on technology for their existence. This group will be a leader when the market begins to turn, up or down. The technology group tends to see the first money spent when companies begin to buy capital equipment such as computers, telephone systems, and electronics. They also feel some of the first budget cuts if companies see their revenues start to slow. You want to own tech when the economy is starting to come out of a slowdown. You definitely want to be out of them when the economy shows weakness. This is a volatile group. These stocks tend to move much more, whether up or down, than most other sectors. You need to own some of these stocks for growth of your investments, but the amount, in terms of a percentage of your portfolio, should reflect your Comfort Zone. A smaller position coincides with investors who don't like to see wild fluctuations in their portfolio values. A good way of owning technology is through mutual funds, where the fund owns many different technology stocks. See chapter 1 for details on mutual funds.

Sector: Utilities

INDUSTRIAL GROUPS: Diversified Utilities, Electric Utilities, Foreign Utilities, Gas Utilities, Water Utilities.

COMMON CHARACTERISTICS: Heavily in debt. All utilities borrow great amounts of money to build and maintain their power plants. That means they're sensitive to the cost of money, which makes them captives of interest rates. When the time comes for a bond (money borrowed) to be paid off (the maturity date), the utility has to either have the cash to make the payment or borrow more money. Almost 100% of the time, utilities will borrow more money. That means they are constantly in the market for more funds. When rates are rising, utilities will pay more for their borrowings. Higher interest payments mean less profits, which can also mean lower dividend payments, though utilities are loath to cut their dividends. But it is a concern, so be aware that utilities that have high debt and use a large percentage of their profits to pay dividends are the ones that will most likely cut them if rates rise too much.

Be Aware of Where Interest Rates Are Going

As I discussed in the last chapter, interest rates are very powerful. They will change the direction of the stock market, and many stocks are very sensitive to the direction rates are moving. In summary, here's what to look for when rates are rising or falling. You'll know it's happening because even the local news covers the Fed now.

When the Fed is moving interest rates higher, all of the financial stocks are adversely affected. Their cost of borrowing money goes up while the price they charge to lend it doesn't move as quickly. Their profit margins are squeezed. Their stock prices go down. So when rates are moving higher avoid financial stocks such as banks, credit card companies, mortgage lenders, savings and loans.

Other groups that are sensitive to interest rates are the home builders and car manufacturers. Most consumers borrow to buy these items. When the cost to borrow goes up, sales in these industries go down. Profits follow. The stocks go down well before sales diminish as investors bail out in anticipation of the slowdown that inevitably follows when rates go higher.

Utilities are also usually poor performers in a higher interest-rate scenario. As mentioned above, they have to borrow a lot of money continuously. As the cost of their debt goes higher, profits diminish.

Basic materials is another group to avoid. Sales in these industries depend on a robust economy. When interest rates are moving up, the economy eventually slows. That's the purpose of higher rates: to slow sales before inflation becomes a problem. When the economy slows, basic materials such as lumber, cement, and steel aren't needed as much. Their sales are directly tied to how the economy is performing. High-interest rates mean lower economic activity.

Technology is another sector that will notice higher interest rates. Like basic materials, sales in this group depend on a robust economy. While you can make the argument that technology increases efficiency and therefore should do well in a slow-growth environment, the reality is that when sales are down, companies don't spend as much on technology. Some technology is exempt from this but, in general, technology is not a great place for investment when the Fed is raising rates.

The last group is the Conglomerates. They're usually so broad-based that any slowdown in the economy from higher rates will hit them in the bottom line.

That leaves several groups that aren't affected by interest rates, and where you should focus your efforts while rates are going up. By the way, when the Fed begins to make a move in interest rates, up or down, it usually takes anywhere from a year to two before they are finished with their efforts. So when the direction of interest rates changes, that's when you want to make changes in your portfolio.

What to Buy When Rates Go Up

The sectors you want to own when rates are going higher are Consumer Goods, Health Care, and Services.

Consumer goods are those products that we all need, no matter where interest rates are, things like toothpaste, food, beverages. We don't care what borrowing costs are because we don't have to borrow to buy these items.

Health Care is another sector impervious to rates. When you're sick, you need drugs. Or you need an operation. You'll buy those no matter what the economy is doing.

Finally, most Services do relatively well during higher-rate environments because their main cost is labor. These companies don't borrow money because there are no assets to buy. Of course, if the economy is slowing, certain service companies will see a drop-off in sales. But they can lay off people, thereby reducing their largest expense. It's not a perfect play for higher-interest rates, but it's strong enough to include for a defensive sector.

What to Buy When Rates Go Lower

If interest rates are going lower, just reverse the above logic. Investors will be very happy to jump into the first group of stocks, the financials, the utilities, etc., the ones that were hurt by the increase in rates. When the Fed starts loosening credit, then those industries will be the first beneficiaries and their bottom lines will increase nicely, especially initially when employers will be reluctant to hire too many people or spend too much on new equipment. They'll want to see if the economy will really improve before they add to payroll. So while their revenues increase, their expenses tend to lag. That adds much more to the bottom line.

That doesn't mean you dump Health Care, Services, and Consumer Goods when rates go down. Rather, you don't add to your positions and sell some of these stocks to fund your new purchases in the industries that will benefit from lower rates. But you definitely do not sell out your defensive stocks. After all, the Fed may only cut rates a few times before it decides to stop and wait to see what happens. Or it may cut rates for years. You never know. No one ever does. That's why you have to stay diversified, to stay balanced, to stay in your Comfort Zone. In chapter 6, I'll describe how to build a portfolio of core holdings that make up a Comfort Zone for any investor.

Now that you have a good description of sectors and industries, you will want to build a portfolio that gives you good diversification. But you may not feel comfortable, at least at the beginning, in buying stocks directly, to develop your own portfolio. Then you'll want to buy mutual funds. There are funds that specialize in each of the sectors: Communication, Financial, Health, Natural Resources, Precious Metals, Real Estate, Technology, Utilities. (I've taken these headings from MSN Money). They are a little different from the headings earlier in the chapter, but I wanted you to see that various resources use different titles for the same basic information. The Web site is http://moneycentral.msn.com/investor/research/fundwelcome.asp?Funds=1.

Keep in mind that each of these funds will only invest in the sector you choose. So you definitely don't want to buy only one. That would put all your money at risk in one sector, which will make you uncomfortable. Ideally, you will buy a little of each of the funds, overweighting the ones that reflect the current state of interest rates.

For example, if rates are going up (as they are while I write this), then you would want to buy more of Health, Communication, Natural Resources, and Precious Metals and less of Financial, Real Estate, and Utilities. But you would still buy a little of the latter group. Remember, no one knows how long the Fed will continue on a certain path, and when it changes, you don't want to be in the wrong sectors with all your money.

You can find a list of the mutual funds in each of these Sector Funds on the above Web site. You can also screen for the top performers that I described in chapter 1. Some of the best funds will have a minimum investment required. Sometimes it's as much as $100,000. Those aren't for you and me. They're for institutions. Fortunately, most funds have a minimum of less than $1,000. For less than $10,000 you can have a portfolio of ten different funds that will give you great diversification and a lot of comfort.

Ways to Invest

There are two ways to invest in particular sectors and industries: directly with stocks and indirectly with mutual funds. Stock investing is a little more demanding and will be covered later. Mutual funds were in chapter 1. Either way, you now have a beginning sense of how to enter your investing Comfort Zone by using different sectors.

PART THREE
BUILD YOUR PORTFOLIO

6

Build Your Core Portfolio

I've got all the money I'll ever need if I die by
four o'clock this afternoon.

—*Henny Youngman*

R isk is not a bad thing. It's like a fast car. It can be dangerous if it's misused. But when properly handled, risk can enhance your returns. You don't have to leave your Comfort Zone to put some risk in your portfolio.

Stocks Come with Risk

There's no getting around it. Investing in stocks or mutual funds or anything other than treasury bills involves risk. But if you only put your money in treasury bills (which mature in less than one year as opposed to notes, which mature in less than ten years, or bonds, which mature in more than ten years), you will never make any real money. In fact, inflation will most likely go up faster than the interest rate you are being paid on your treasury bills. That means you lose purchasing power in the long run—basically, you lose money with this strategy.

Don't get me wrong. Buying Treasury bills is fine, if you need money within a year. You don't want to risk those funds. They're a good place to invest when you absolutely have to have your principal returned in a short period of time. Think of them as a parking place, though, not as a permanent residence for your money.

This is a fact: You have to take some risk if you're going to make money. But that doesn't mean you have to do something outside your Comfort Zone. It does mean you have to go beyond the shallow end of the pool.

What Risk Is

First, if you understand the nature of risk, as it applies to investing, it will help you determine where you are most comfortable. The "no-risk" proposition in investing is the Treasury bill. It has the lowest interest rate because you are guaranteed by the Federal government that you will get your money back when the Treasury bill matures. For our purposes here, let's assume that bills maturing in 3 months yield 3%. That means if you buy $1,000 worth of bills for three months, at the end of three months, you'll have earned ¼ of 3% or .75 basis points. Remember, the 3% is for the full year and three months is only a quarter of that time period. If you bought a bill that matured in 1 year, you'd have $30 of interest at the end of the year. (If you would like to buy bills directly from the government, you can go to www.treasurydirect.gov. You set up an account online and buy the bills, notes, or bonds directly from the Treasury with no commissions.)

So in this example, the least risk you can take will reward you with 3%. That's our base risk level. If you want to take more risk, such as buying a Treasury note that matures in 5 years, it may pay 4%. If you buy a corporate note (one where a corporation will pay the interest over the 5 years, not the government), you might get 4.5%, but you'll be taking more risk because the company doesn't have the creditworthiness of the federal government. That's why they have to pay more for your money. You're getting rewarded for the added risk you're taking.

You've now got two elements of risk working: longer time and less certainty for repayment. A longer time means you get paid more because you could always buy the 3-month Treasury bill and reinvest the proceeds with no risk every 3 months. To invest for a longer period of time, you need an incentive, which is the higher rate. If you buy the corporate issue, you're adding more uncertainty as to the payment at maturity. If you were to buy a longer-term Treasury or corporate bond, say a 10-year note, your reward would be even higher because you're adding more time and more risk. That's on the bond side of life.

The Stock Side of Risk

When you enter the stock side of investing, then you're adding even more risk. There are no guarantees here. In the bond world, you are buying a promise from the government, or a company, that it will pay you back all your investment at the maturity date of the bond, plus interest owed. There is the full faith and credit of the U.S. government backing the promise on the treasuries. Sometimes there are assets backing the promise from companies. When you buy stock in companies, you have no promise of anything. So there is, by definition, higher risk to stock investing.

What you are doing when you buy stock is allying yourself with the other owners of a company. You are willing to lose more for the chance of gaining more. Instead of a fixed amount, which is what you'd be paid in the form of interest if you own a bond, you will participate in the gains the company makes in the form of a higher return on your equity (meaning the profits that go to the bottom line are owned by all shareholders and when times are good, they are much more than the interest paid on a bond). Conversely, if there are losses, the equity will diminish, and you will be poorer because of it since you, as a shareholder, own the equity. If the stock pays a dividend, you may get a higher dividend when profits increase or the dividend may decrease if there are losses.

The point here is that owning stocks increases your risk. By definition, that means, if you're totally risk averse, you may be leaving your Comfort Zone by owning them. But not all stocks are equally risky, and there are ways to diminish the risk but not to eliminate it. Some readers, however, will have a very high comfort level for risk and want to increase it. You can do that by not following the ideas given in this book. But be aware that increasing your risk level will most likely decrease your wealth.

Developing Your Core Portfolio

If you accept the premise that investing is risky, then you have to diminish the risk as best you can to stay in your Comfort Zone. Two major components of the strategy are (1) buy the best stocks, and (2) diversify. Nothing new here. But some people don't know exactly what that means. It means you buy the strongest, most profitable company in an industry group, and that you diversify among many industry groups, as described in chapter 5. Below is a Core Portfolio that will give you both the quality and diversification you need.

Following are the stocks and/or funds you should buy in order to minimize your risk, maximize your Comfort Zone, *and* make money.

Buy These

1. **An oil stock.** While oil seems to be at a high point at this writing, it's hard to make a case for the black stuff going back to $30 a share. That's because China needs much more than it's getting if it's going to continue strong economic growth. It will want even more as more cars are brought into their economy. Buy one of the biggest and financially strongest in this sector and hold on. It will have some ups and downs, but the dividends will be safe. Leading candidates would be ExxonMobil and Chevron. Again, don't buy these as soon as you read this. These stocks may be way overpriced or have had significant changes since I've written this. The idea is to buy the strongest of the strong. These two are currently in that category.

2. **A tech stock.** Technology brings higher productivity. There will always be a need for better technology. Pick one of the large-cap innovators, the one that has a core product such as semiconductors or software that many other tech companies need. These are more volatile and go through cycles so be prepared for large stock price moves, up and down. Ideas: Intel, Microsoft, and Cisco Systems. (Remember: Do not just buy these stocks because they're listed here. You will need to check their value to determine if they still warrant inclusion in your portfolio.)

3. **An index fund.** These are funds that track certain groups of stocks such as the Standard and Poor's 500, the Dow Jones Industrial Average, or the Russell 2000. Pick one of the index funds that tracks the large-cap stocks. That way you'll have part of your portfolio in the biggest and best companies in the United States. The easiest way to buy an index fund, such as the S&P 500, is through a stocklike instrument on the American Exchange called a SPYDER. The symbol is SPY. Another fund that trades like a stock is QQQQ. It represents the 100 largest stocks on the NASDAQ. These are called exchange-traded funds or ETFs. Many of the index funds are traded as ETFs. A great resource for learning about and finding index funds is at www.indexfunds.com.

4. **A large drug company.** Drugs are the most efficient way to treat many diseases. The large drug companies have strong cash flows, and the best ones have promising new drugs in the pipeline. Pick one that has a good dividend and isn't currently in the courtroom in a prominent way. Or you can take a little more risk and buy one that is. Most of them have very secure dividends. Some of the best are Merck (even with Vioxx suits), Pfizer, and Eli Lilly. But these stocks could have gone through major changes when you read this so investigate each of them before you invest.

5. **A large biotech company.** While the large drug companies are curing many diseases, the cures for cancer and other viruses will most likely come from the biotechs. Again, stay with the proven winners, the ones that have strong revenues and healthy profits. There aren't many of them, but the ones that have delivered should continue to do so for some time. The unquestionable leader of this pack is Amgen with Genentech not far behind.

6. **One stock from the Dow Jones Industrial Average.** As of this writing, the DJIA has these stocks in it: Alcoa—AA; American Express—AXP; AT&T—T; Boeing—BA; Caterpillar—CAT; Coca-Cola—KO; Citigroup—C; Disney—DIS; DuPont—DD; Eastman Kodak—EK; ExxonMobil—XOM; General Electric—GE; General

Motors—GM; Hewlett-Packard—HWP; Home Depot—HD; Honeywell—HON; IBM—IBM; Intel—INTC; International Paper—IP; Johnson & Johnson—JNJ; McDonald's—MCD; Merck—MRK; Microsoft—MSFT; 3M—MMM; JP Morgan—JPM; Altria—MO; Proctor & Gamble—PG; SBC Communications—SBC; United Tech—UTX; Wal-Mart—WMT.

Don't just randomly pick one. Maybe the best one for you is the one with the highest dividend. Maybe you don't want to own a tobacco company, so don't choose Altria (previously Phillip Morris). Maybe you're concerned about interest rates going higher, so don't buy Citigroup. In other words, you'll have to look at each one individually and decide the one that makes the most sense to you based on current economic conditions. These stocks are some of the biggest and the best.

7. **One brand-name stock.** Pick a well-known name like Coca-Cola, McDonald's, Disney, Tide (owned by Procter & Gamble), or Nike. A highly recognizable brand name has a competitive advantage in every market. Choose one you buy all the time and investigate its financials fully. You can bet you're not the only one using that brand. Of course, it will have to be a different one from the stock you chose from the Dow Jones Industrial Average or any of the previous categories.

8. **A consumer staples stock.** These are the basics like soap, toothpaste, deodorant, razor blades, things that are quickly consumed and bought again. No matter what the economy does, people will buy these products. Good examples are Procter & Gamble, Colgate, Clorox, Church & Dwight (makes Arm & Hammer baking soda), and Tupperware.

9. **An emerging technology.** Every one wants to own the next Microsoft. The odds of doing it are more than 10,000 to 1 if you buy just one stock. But if you buy a technology fund that specializes in small-cap stocks (the new ones), you'll have better odds. You can find specialized funds by using mutual-fund screening programs on

AOL, Yahoo!Finance, MSNMoney, and other financial sites. The current technology buzz is big on nanotechnology and wi-fi. Which companies will finally deliver is the big question. By owning a specialized tech fund, you don't have to know. You can have a small part of many of the new technology stocks with one fund. Some examples with good track records at the time of this writing: Ivy Science & Technology Fund "A" (WSTAX); Ivy Science & Technology Fund "Y" (WSTYX); Waddell & Reed Advisor Science and Technology Fund "A" (UNSCX); and Waddell & Reed Advisor Science and Technology Fund "Y' (USTFX). All of these have a 5-star rating from Morningstar (the highest). But this isn't nearly enough information for you to buy them. You need to see what their fees are, what their returns are when you're reading this, what types of stocks they buy, etc. I found these in less than a minute by using the Yahoo!Finance Mutual Fund Screening program (http://screen .yahoo.com/funds.html). I chose: Specialized-Technology as my fund category; chose "Any" for Fund Family; picked Top 10% for the Rank in Category; I wanted a fund manager who'd been there awhile so I clicked on "Longer than 5 years" for the "Manager Tenure"; chose a Morningstar rating of 5 (Best), and then let the program find the funds that matched those criteria. Only four did. To find more funds, I could change those parameters and see what others came up. Then I would fully investigate each fund before buying.

10. **One dividend stock or income fund.** This is a holding that will throw off cash in good times and bad. If you opt for one stock, make sure the dividend will be paid through economic cycles. That means finding a stock that pays less than 50% of its income out for the dividend. Also, don't reach just for the dividend. In other words, if the average dividend is about 2%, be suspicious of something that is yielding 8% or higher. Higher yields mean higher risks. If you're only going for the dividend, check out Real Estate Investment Trusts and Utilities. If you want the dividend and some growth, check out a large-cap stock like General Electric. If you opt for an income

fund, pick one that has stocks, not bonds. In fact, bond funds that specialize in longer maturities will have a rough time if interest rates go higher. You'll have more yield, but your principal will be at risk as bond prices move lower. If you're going to buy a bond fund, pick one that is short term or intermediate term in maturity, the ones that mature in 5 years or less. A description of the fund from any quote program will tell you this information.

Investments That Work in Good Times and Bad

If you buy these ten different types of investments, you'll have an excellent core portfolio, one that will withstand the ravages of the stock market. As mentioned before, you don't just buy and forget these funds and stocks. You have to monitor what they're doing, how their earnings are growing, changes taking place in your funds. But be reluctant to sell your holdings once you've picked excellent ones. Think of giving them each at least a year before you make a decision on whether to move to another stock or fund in the same category. Chances are if you're buying the best of each type, whatever the problem your stock or fund is having is affecting all the other stocks and funds in the group. Winning comfortably in the investment race is a marathon, not a sprint. Be prepared to hold on, through good times and bad.

There is another reason to hold the biggest and best: When times are bad, they'll feel it the least because they can adapt better. Smaller stocks or weaker ones don't have the capital cushion to ride out the storms. Stick with the great stocks. You need very good reasons for selling any of them.

How—and How Much—to Buy

To buy stocks, you need to use a brokerage firm. These are covered in chapter 13 as are ways to buy mutual funds. As to how much to buy of each category, you have to be disciplined about it and put 10% of your investable funds in each one. That means you first buy the mutual funds. That gives you diversity and professional management right away.

Remember that this is money set aside for investing. That means you've got savings for at least six months of living expenses and your credit cards are paid off. In fact, make it a priority to pay off your credit cards. You won't find investments that pay as much as the credit cards charge for interest. Get rid of the credit card debt. Then save for a rainy day. You can cheat a little if you've saved enough for three months and will continue to save until you get to six months, but the emphasis in this book is finding your Comfort Zone. There are no short cuts to the Comfort Zone, and if you don't pay off credit cards or have those savings, you will definitely be way out of the zone.

Once you buy the funds and/or stocks, assume you can't touch them for five years. Of course, as mentioned earlier, if something changes within the companies or funds, you can sell them and buy others. But if you are going to invest and to make money, you have to have patience. In fact, patience is so rare in investing that it has the highest reward. Warren Buffett, the best investor ever, likes to say that his favorite holding period is forever. And he's a very, very, very rich man.

Buy the mutual funds first, then individual stocks. You should monitor the individual stocks for news, which you can do in a few minutes every day on your computer by simply getting a quote for the stock from one of the main sites already listed. Below the quote for a stock is the news headlines or a link to the news about the stocks. Unless there is a major, major problem with a stock, such as the accounting has been wrong for years due to dishonesty or something dramatically destructive has happened, don't be in a hurry to sell a stock. One bad quarter doesn't mean you get out. It does mean you monitor it and see how the company is doing and if it's correcting the problems. If you're buying the best stock in an industry, it will most likely rebound from any temporary problems or adjust its practices to correct them.

As for mutual funds, check them every quarter at least. They shouldn't move too much day to day, but the general trend should be higher over a year's period. If you've lost money over three years, you definitely should get out of a fund. But to judge a solid, well-performing fund on one quarter or even one year isn't the right time frame. You have to let the management adjust to whatever is causing the market to do poorly. Again, you're buying well-diversified, large stock funds. They won't make you rich overnight so they won't make you poor overnight either. Give them time to work. If you've chosen a strong performing fund that has delivered solid returns over many years, it should continue to do so based on its investing philosophy. Give it time.

Since you have bought both your stocks and your funds wisely, once you own them you don't have to check their prices every hour, or even every day. That's certainly the case for the funds. But you should check your stocks for news. That's part of your job. But it shouldn't make you anxious. It should just be part of investing, and as you learn more about your companies it should be fun, too.

Managing Your Core Portfolio

When you've established your ten basic holdings, you'll have to watch each of them for news and price activity. Tracking your stocks is easy. Market-Watch will e-mail you any news on a stock if you sign up for the service. Or you can simply look at most quote programs and the headlines on the stock, which are listed below the quote for the stock.

What you're looking for is meaningful changes in a company. In other words, if a new large contract is announced with large revenues in the future, that's a great bit of news. If, however, the company announces they've decided to repaint their buildings, it won't have an impact. If the news is good, then enjoy the upward move in the stock. If the news is bad, you need to think it through.

Bad news can be many things. It can represent a one time event such as a natural disaster interrupting power for a week. Or it can be the beginning of many damaging announcements that will continue for months to come. The problem is, you never know if the first news is only the tip of the iceberg. Usually, if there is an accounting problem, such that earnings have to be restated, that can be a warning of worse things to come, particularly if the accounting change was due to fraud. That's almost always trouble for a long time.

Every news item has to be examined for its possible long-term impact on the stock. Don't be too quick to want to get out of a stock, especially these best of breed winners that you've picked. It would take outright fraud or extreme adverse economic conditions to damage them permanently. Be reluctant to sell any of your core holdings, even if they go through a quarter or two of bad times.

Give each stock and mutual fund at least one year before you decide to sell it unless two things happen: there is definite fraud in the way it does business (highly unlikely for these companies) or the stock or mutual fund represents more than 20% of your holdings. In other words, it has increased in value to a point where it dominates the portfolio. When it gets to that level (and this is nice problem to have), sell half the position to get it back to 10% and if it's really on a winning streak, it will once again grow to 20% and you can sell half again. It's a good thing.

Beyond the Core: Ways to Take Risk

If you want to go beyond the core portfolio, take some additional risk, then put 90% of your investable funds in the above categories and use the last 10% to go a little crazy but not so much that you move out of your Comfort Zone. A little more risk can bring big rewards, but it can also cost you. So be careful. Here are some ways to take more risk without being too risky.

1. **Buy a busted blue chip.** It seems like there is always a great stock that hits some bad times. As I write this Merck is slogging through the Vioxx lawsuits. The stock has been punished for bringing a drug to market without fully disclosing the side effects. But it's paying a 5.2% dividend that is extremely safe for the next 10 years, even if it pays out $1 billion a year in settlements. It has a strong enough cash flow to cover the dividend payments and the legal claims. I own the stock because I believe it will settle the lawsuits, win some and lose some, and finally return to focusing on its large pipeline of new drugs. This is a bit of a risk but one that seems to me worth taking.

2. **Buy a biotech mutual fund.** While the core portfolio describes buying a biotech stock that is the leader in the field, this risk-taking idea allows you maybe, just maybe, to own a company that will deliver the next breakthrough drug or vaccine. Because you need to have a very

diverse group of biotech stocks in order to capture the one or two that will finally make it successfully, a mutual fund is the only way to go. You can find a list of them and their track records by using one of the mutual fund screening programs already described. Choose the category: "Specialized Fund—Biotechnology" to see a list.

3. **Buy an aggressive growth fund.** These funds buy the newer, smaller companies. You don't want to try this at home because, just like in biotech, many of these companies don't go from small to big. They go from small to gone. But if you can get professional stock pickers and good diversification, you've got a chance of making some money in this treacherous area of the market. Use the fund screening program to find these under the names of Aggressive Growth or Small Cap Funds.

4. **Invest in a local company that isn't public.** This is really risky but sometimes the best investments are literally in our own backyards. You can't get your money out of an investment like this unless there's a buyout or the stock goes public, or you have an agreement with the owner on how you can get it out (something I strongly suggest do *before* you invest your money). You can find these gems by talking with friends and family and letting it be known that you're interested in looking at start-up businesses. You will get lots of proposals. Make sure you look at them carefully, especially the part about how the new company is going to make revenues and when, as well as profits. Or you can approach a successful business in your community and see if it's looking to expand. Most of the time additional capital is welcome. Again, remember that you only want to put, at the most, 10% of your investing dollars in something like this. It's easy to believe the sky's the limit as the owner excitedly explains his or her plans.

How to tell if the company has good management? Here's what Warren Buffett says about the management of companies he buys. "I look for three things in the company management: honesty, hard work, and intelligence. If they don't have the first one, the other two will kill you."

5. **Buy a local company that is already public.** You know more about
    a business in your community than any analyst will, at least in the
    first few years. Here are a few that started locally: Starbucks, Mc-
    Donald's, Home Depot, Wal-Mart. The list is long and impressive. If
    you've got a hot store in your area or a new machine that is made in
    your town that has back orders for the next two years, then maybe it
    will be a national hit. Or maybe it will just be prosperous in your
    state. If it's doing well where you are, chances are it will do well else-
    where. Again, you have to do some homework to find these gems,
    but ask around your town, then do your homework. You might dis-
    cover a real treasure.

    Those are five ways to take higher risk than the Core Portfolio.
    Some of them take a little more work than the large stocks or mu-
    tual funds. But their rewards can be enormous. As I described ear-
    lier, I found a small, local company through a friend, invested in it
    at $8 and watched it go to $113. Those are very rare, but they do
    happen. (I've also heard some ideas from friends, invested in them
    at $10, and watched them go to 0, but that's another story—actually
    many more stories.)

Take Risks That Fit Your Personality

Part of the secret of staying in your Comfort Zone is to understand who
you are as an investor. Going back to our swimming pool analogy, some of
you will only be comfortable if you're sitting in a chair on the pool deck
fully dressed. Then you shouldn't invest in any stocks or funds. Just buy
treasuries and understand that you will never make money, but you'll never
see monetary losses either. You just won't buy as much in ten years as
everyone else will who invested properly. In other words, the purchasing
power of your money will be much less because the value of your investments, in real terms, will go down.

If you've at least got your swimsuit on and sit on the edge, feet dangling
in the water, watching others, you can buy mutual funds that specialize in
short maturity bonds.

If you're able to walk down the steps into the pool, and move around in the shallow end, then you've got a chance to make some money. You can buy mutual funds that are split between large-cap stocks and bonds.

If you're willing to swim to the middle of the pool, buy mutual funds and large-cap stocks knowing that there's some risk, but you can still touch the bottom.

If you're comfortable with some risk, willing to give up the bottom and the sides of the pool and swim freely in the deep end, then go for the Core Portfolio. You'll have more fun and make more money.

Finally, if you're the person who heads for the ten-foot diving board, jumps as high as you can, then dives elegantly into the pool, go for it all. Buy the Core Portfolio and make at least two of the more risky investments described above. You'll definitely have the most fun, but you'll also have to live with the most stress because those risky investments don't always pay off. But when they do, you can buy your own pool.

7

Six Elements of Great Stocks

When a stock doubles, sell it.
If it doesn't double, don't buy it.

—*Will Rogers*

N ow that you've got ideas for a Core Portfolio, you'll need some criteria for finding the best stocks to buy. The best stocks can be subjective because different investors have different objectives. My objective is to put you in your Comfort Zone. That means buying stocks that have the following characteristics, those common to most great stocks.

Great Management

You have to start at the top. That means the people who run the business: management. Management is not the board of directors. Directors are important, but they aren't involved in the day-to-day running of the business. Their job is to oversee what management does and protect shareholders. Management is mostly the chief executive officer, the president, the chief operating officer, and the chief financial officer. These are people responsible for executing the business plan for a company. They make most of the decisions. They are the key to any business's success.

Great management is hard to find. In fact, Mike Milken, one of the great financial minds of our time, used to say that there is never a shortage of capital, only a shortage of good management. In other words, money will always be invested in companies with good people running them, people who know how to manage capital well.

There are ways to tell how good management is. The first one is consistency of earnings. If a company is continually reporting earnings that are improving, over a period of years, it's because management is taking care of business. Good earnings growth doesn't happen by chance (though it can happen in different ways that I'll go into later). Study the last several years of a company's earnings, and see if they've been heading higher. You can view past earnings in any annual report or on most Web sites that give quotes. Of course, if the economy has been weak, it's hard to improve earnings, but some companies manage to do it. Again, it doesn't happen by chance; the management is making sure it happens. Then, dishonest management will show earnings growth as well—look at Enron under Ken Lay and MCI under Bernard Ebbers or Tyco under Dennis Kozlowski.

Good management is forthright with its shareholders. They tell about problems that are developing or surprises that will affect this quarter's or year's earnings. While there are laws that require such disclosure, not all management complies. When silent management announces earnings, sometimes there's a bad surprise.

Honesty is a big part of good management. In addition to being forthright, these managers tend to live by the UPOD rule: Under Promise, Over Deliver. In other words, when they give guidance for next quarter's earnings or next year's, they tend to be cautious rather than optimistic. They'd rather paint a realistic picture that allows for a pleasant surprise. Admittedly, this is a hard trait to know about management. If investors had been able to see this one easily, all of them could have avoided disasters like Enron, Tyco, Adelphia, and MCI.

To see a few managers who have delivered for shareholders, watch John Chambers of Cisco Systems or Jeff Immelt of GE or Craig Barrett of Intel or—best of all—Warren Buffett of Berkshire Hathaway. There are many others who tell it like it is, and usually add a little optimism if possible. But they don't try to impress with hype. They stick to the reality of their companies, the economy as they see it, and how they will adapt to the current environment.

Another attribute of great management is a commitment to grow. Although growth is one of the six elements of great stocks and the next one I'll describe, it's the mind-set of management to grow that I'm addressing here. Great companies continue to grow, either by trying new products, which sometimes fail, or by buying other, less efficient companies that are then streamlined and contribute to the bottom line, or by constantly expanding markets for their products. If management isn't committed to growing the company, it won't, and neither will the stock price.

You can find out about management of most companies by checking their Web sites, getting the names of the officers, and then doing a search on the Web. There are plenty of articles about most corporate officers. You can also read about their backgrounds in filings with the SEC, especially the annual proxy statements at www.sec.gov.

Great Growth

Growth occurs because management has the nerve to fail. It takes a certain personality to try something new and watch it flop. That's what happens to many new products introduced every year. If management only stuck to what the company is currently doing, it would ultimately fail. Because every company has competition, and the competition is working on ways to be more efficient, to lower prices, to take all the business. That's the way business works.

Management has to be committed to growing the business or it will not succeed. How they grow the business is just as important. For example, many companies grow only through acquisitions. That's not the best kind of growth because many of those don't work out. Or the cultures of the two firms clash; and though they aren't failures alone, the two companies never really mesh. Plus most acquisitions are not immediately positive for a company's bottom line because of costs associated with the purchase and ongoing liabilities brought along with the new company.

That's not to say a company that grows through acquisitions is doing the wrong thing. In fact, some companies are known as consolidators, and they usually do well. Consolidators take a very specialized industry, one that is usually run by a local group, and buys that local company, brings efficiencies to it that only a large company can, and incorporates it into a larger, national service or product. An example would be the funeral business or a garbage dump or dry cleaning or local transportation companies such as freight forwarders. If you find a consolidator, then growth by acquisition is natural and usually positive.

But if you're looking at a large company that is buying its way into new businesses, watch out. The management is definitely growing the business by adding new revenues, but because it has little or no experience in these new fields, it will most likely not bring any efficiencies and/or management expertise to those companies. You'll see this in companies trying to become a conglomerate. They've been very successful in one market, so they take their stock or large cash positions, and start buying into other, less profitable sectors. That rarely works out.

What you are looking for most of all is internal growth. This is the good kind of growth. It comes from making more widgets more efficiently and selling more of them. In other words, as the company grows, it is getting more profitable because of that efficiency. That shows that management knows what it's doing by continually driving down the costs and broadening the market for its product. The natural evolution for internal growth is to develop products that go with the core business, such as printers that go with computers (see Dell) or fries that go with burgers (see McDonalds') or special software that goes with operating systems (see Microsoft) or bottled water when soda has been your strength (see Coca-Cola).

When you find a company that is growing, both in revenues and profits, and the profits are growing faster than the revenues, be very reluctant to ever sell it. These stocks have a way of going up and up and up over many decades. See each of the above mentioned companies as good examples.

Great ROE

No, this isn't caviar. It refers to Return on Equity. Equity is what you own when you buy a stock. You are looking for a high return on your investment. What the company makes as net income or net profits is added to your equity. That is your return on equity. It's measured as a percentage, such as 10% ROE. ROE is reportedly Warren Buffett's favorite number. That's how important it is.

Let's look at a company's balance sheet for a moment to understand this concept. One part is the liabilities of a company or what it owes. (The other side is the assets, what it owns.) Part of the liability side is debt, part of it is current payments owed, and part of it is equity, because the company owes that to the shareholders. That's you if you buy the stock. You're looking for that equity number to grow because that's what you can claim as yours.

In this hypothetical company, let's say it has $1,000 of equity and you buy 1% of the company for $10. If the company makes $100 in a year, then your share of that profit is $1. You've made 10% on your investment. That's a pretty good return when compared to other investments but then you're taking more risk. The company might have lost $100 and your $10 would only be worth $9, but let's make this a happy example.

You can see that if the company were to continue to earn 10% a year, the magic of compounding interest would make you very wealthy. The next year it would earn $110 for another 10% return and so forth. And that's what you can look for in the best companies: a continued high return on equity (ROE). Examples of strong ROE companies are:

- **Accenture Limited (a consulting firm) (ACN-NYSE).** In the last five years, it has shown a ROE of 45.5%, 46.9%, 62.7%, 136.2%, and 308.1%.

- **Coca-Cola.** Over the last 5 years, ROE has been 15%, 16.2%, 18.16%, 17.9%, and 19.3%. (These are remarkable numbers because it's very hard for large companies to continue to show high ROE numbers. The bigger they get, the more equity they have, the larger the base number is for the percentage growth. That's why very high ROE stocks are usually smaller or medium-sized companies.)

- **NVR, Inc. (home builder).** ROE for the last five years: 56%, 62.7%, 84.8%, 82.2%, and 67.8%.

- **Yum! Brands (owner of Kentucky Fried Chicken, Pizza Hut, and Taco Bell).** For the last five years, ROE has been 34%, 41.6%, 56.1%, 98.1%, and 473.1%.

- **Zimmer Holdings (maker of orthopedic products).** ROE for the last five years, 16%, 15.2%, 9.3%, 70.4%, and 242%.

I found these in the *Value Line Investment Survey,* in the "Index to Stocks" supplement. It has a list of high ROE companies every week. You can also find the ROE in the fundamental information on most stocks from stock quote programs. In AOL's stock screening program, you can find stocks based on ROE.

Please keep this in mind: DO NOT BUY A STOCK BASED ON ONE NUMBER. As you can see from the above examples, the ROE will fluctuate, especially in the early years of a company. Zimmer Holdings had an astronomical ROE of 242% five years ago, but it had just been formed two years previous to that and went public in the same year. It's exciting to see a return on your investment of 242% but it isn't realistic to expect a company to continue those results. In fact, if a company can make 15% or higher ROE every year, that's a strong indication of good management. It's the ability to continuously deliver a high ROE that you want to find, not one-year wonders.

Also, the ROE increase does not mean the stock will go up by the same amount. Zimmer Holdings stock didn't double the year it reported the high ROE, but it did more than triple over the next three years. A high ROE will be reflected in the stock's price but not in a direct one-to-one relationship, and not immediately. Investors want to see if the ROE is for real, meaning they will be cautious initially about a very high number but buy very strongly if a high ROE is continuously reported.

Great PSR

PSR stands for Price to Sales Ratio. Think of it as a macro way to measure a stock. It tells you how much you are paying for the sales or revenue of a company.

Let's say a company is selling $100,000 of a product. That's total sales.

And the company has 100,000 shares outstanding and selling at $1. The PSR for this stock would be 1.

To calculate a PSR, you determine the sales for a company. In this case there is $100,000. Then you divide that by the number of shares. There are 100,000 shares here. This gives you the sales per share. The last step is to take the price of the stock and divide it by the sales per share. The price here is $1 and the sales per share is $1—1 divided by 1 is 1, so the PSR is 1.

If we had the same company selling $500,000' worth of stuff with the same number of shares, the sales per share would be $5. If the stock were trading at $1, then the PSR would be .2 (1/5). If the stock were trading at $20, then the PSR would be 4 (20/5).

The lower the PSR, the better your chances of success. Remember this is what you are paying for—the *sales* of a company, not the profits. (You don't have to do the PSR math. The Web sites already cited will give you the PSRs of any stock, but it helps to know how to calculate it.) Having a low PSR doesn't mean much by itself unless you know what the industry average is for the stock you're investigating.

In the grocery business, a PSR of .5 isn't unusual. Grocery stores don't get high valuations for their sales. A software company like Microsoft has a PSR of 8 as of this writing. That's because investors believe there is still plenty of room for growth at this company as opposed to an Albertson's (a national grocery store) with a PSR of .23. The competitiveness of groceries is much fiercer than well-protected software programs. So you have to determine what the average PSR for an industry is before you know if a particular stock is being valued well above or below the rest of its competition.

This valuation should make intuitive sense to you. If were to buy the corner gas station, you would want to know how much revenue it's bringing in. That would help you determine what price you'd pay. (Of course, you'd want to know the profits as well, but the amount of sales is important.) If it was bringing in $50,000 a year in sales, you probably would be hard-pressed to pay $300,000 for it, knowing that profits are pretty slim from the strong competition in gas stations.

The same is true for any stock you consider. Knowing how much revenue per share helps you with a reality check. You don't want to overpay for a stock any more than you want to overpay for a gas station. Check the PSR in the quote programs, and then check that PSR against the industry by using the "Competitors" or "Comparison" link.

Here's how to do that. Go to the Yahoo!Finance site given earlier. Put in the symbol ABS and get the quote. On the quote page, you'll see what the price is. On the left side there is a link to Competitors. Click on that. You'll see Albertson's PSR. (They use P/S instead of PSR but it's the same thing.) When I looked Albertson's had a PSR of .23. The competition given is Kroger (.26), Walgreen (1.10), and Wal-Mart (.62) with the Industry Average at .25. So Albertson's has a PSR below its competition as well as a little bit less than the Industry Average. If you like the other elements of the company, this would be one more positive reason to buy the stock.

Microsoft, on the other hand, has a different standing in its competitive landscape. Its PSR is 8 (at this writing). Its competitors (as given in the program) show 1.33 at IBM, 5.83 at Oracle, and 1.21 at SunMicro Systems with the Industry Average at 2.34. So if Mister Softie (Microsoft) is on your shopping list, you'd have to find a lot of other good reasons for buying the stock because the PSR is definitely very high.

As mentioned before, one data point does not make a decision for you. You may think MSFT has such a strong position in software that it deserves a high PSR, and you wouldn't be alone. It's just that the focus here is on your Comfort Zone and helping you get into it with real numbers. A high PSR will often signal a stock price that can't be sustained. But you need to view any PSR within the context of its industry.

As an added comment on Microsoft, it has always carried a high PSR. Companies with monopolies, or something like a monopoly, always do. As long as the company grew its revenues at higher than normal increases, investors were comfortable. As revenue growth has slowed, the PSR has diminished because it's hard to believe MSFT can continue high revenue growth when it's already bringing in $40 billion a year (as of this writing).

Low PSRs can give plenty of comfort to investors. The lower the number, the less you're paying for the revenues of the company.

Great Profitability

Revenues are great but they don't mean anything if they're not turned into profits. In fact, it's the profits that investors get to keep. That's why profits are the key ingredient to a great stock. And unlike a PSR, the higher the number you can find for profitability, the better.

Profits are what's left over after all the expenses of a company are paid. If a company brings in $100 in revenues and pays out $95 in total expenses on labor, rent, depreciation of equipment, freight charges, utility bills, advertising and incidentals, then it made $5 in profits. That $5 is kept in the company and can be used to grow the business by buying more equipment, or pay a dividend, or buy back stock, or it can simply be held until a good opportunity arises. This little company is making a 5% net profit ($5 of profits divided by $100 of revenues).

Now all you have to do is multiply the revenue numbers by some large amount, and you're in the real world. Right now the largest company in the United States is ExxonMobil, the oil company. It has revenues of $312 billion. It has a net profit margin of 9.6%, as of this writing, calculated the same way we did the $100 company above. (The net profit margin is a way of expressing profits as a percentage of revenues. That makes it easy to compare companies. Use the net profit margin to determine which is the most efficient provider of the goods or service within an industry. Again, the Web sites already mentioned will list the Net Profit Margins and industry comparisons.) The higher the net profit margin percentage, the better.

Here are profit margins from a few well-known companies in their latest fiscal year: Microsoft, 32%; Wal-Mart, 3.6%; General Motors, 1.9%; Coca-Cola, 22.8%; McDonald's, 12.4%; Starbucks, 7.4%; Boeing, 2.5%; Amgen, 27.3%.

You can see for these specific years, there is a wide divergence in profitability among these large companies. General Motors had a tough time, squeezing out almost 2% profitability while Microsoft scored the highest with 32%. Does that mean you simply buy Microsoft and ignore all the others?

By now, you know that buying a stock based on one number won't put you in your Comfort Zone. Also, buying only one stock is never the right move. You need to look at profit margins in two ways: in the context of the competition, and the trend of profitability. The easiest way to do that is to use two resources: a Web site such as MSNMoney Central that gives the profit margin for each company in an industry, and *Value Line* for the trend in the profit margin.

Let's look at the beverage industry where Coca-Cola competes. By going to www.moneycentral.msn.com/investor/finder/customstocksdl.asp, you'll find a screening program. The first box is for the industry. Open the box and click on Beverages—Soft Drinks. Ignore all the other boxes for a moment and go down to the one called Net Profit Margin. Open that and choose "As high as possible." Now go to the bottom of the page and click on Search.

Within a few seconds you'll see a list of stocks, ranked from the highest to lowest for net profit margin and the amount of the net profit margin. On the day I did the screen, Coca-Cola was at the top and showed 21.6%. The next soft-drink maker was Hansen Natural Company with 15%. There were 16 companies listed, including 7 foreign companies. The lowest net profit margin was 1.5%.

As investors, we're most interested in the "best of breed" stocks for our Core Portfolio. Coca-Cola certainly qualifies on many different counts. Now we know its net profit margin is the highest in the industry, and there's one more reason to make it a candidate for the Core Portfolio.

The second consideration, the trend of the profit margin, is found in *Value Line*. On the page with Coca-Cola information, near the middle of the table of numbers is the line for Net Profit Margin. For Coca-Cola, it shows data since 1989. If we look at just the last 5 years, to see how the trend has gone, we see 17.9%, 22.7%, 21%, 22.8%, and 22.8%. Not really a trend as much as a consistently high level of profits, which is to be expected in a mature company like Coke. The fact that it continues to have these strong numbers is a testament to the management of the company.

What you ideally will find is an increasing net profit margin, especially as a company is growing its revenues. That says the company is getting more efficient as it grows, getting more profits from each incremental dollar of sales. Again, that's the ideal. Those companies are hard to find, but with the use of *Value Line* (or the company's own reports), you can find the net profit margin and its trend.

Be aware of the distinction between small, medium, and large companies when you are judging the trend. A smaller, newer company will have many start-up costs that will hurt net profit margin. A medium-size company should have a better trend because it is over the initial hurdles and expenses of a new company. Look for the best trends in this group. Large companies will have the challenge of finding new ways of cutting costs to increase the bottom line. But great companies find a way to do it.

Focus on profitability, not so much from an absolute dollar perspective because earning a billion dollars at ExxonMobil would be a terrible year but a great one for Shoeshine Inc. It's the net profit margin that tells the story for investors. How much is the company able to keep from the revenues it's producing? The more it keeps, the better the ROE. And that's what really counts for investors because the equity is what they own.

High Management Ownership

You want management and directors owning a lot of stock. It means they'll do everything they can to make the company a huge success. It's in their selfish interest. There is a virtue in this type of selfishness if you're a shareholder as well.

Here again you need some perspective. No investor expects the management or board of directors at IBM to own a large percentage of shares. That would be impossible because there are so many shares outstanding. This is a huge company. But in a smaller company, even a medium-sized one (say $1 billion to $3 billion in market cap), investors like to see management and directors with a meaningful percentage of the stock. In this context, 10% to 20% would be significant.

The more stock management and directors own, the more focused on cost cutting they will be. Maybe the company doesn't really need a Gulfstream jet. It's an expensive perk. If there's high stock ownership internally, you can be sure expenditures like these would be hotly debated. Why waste the money on a private plane when commercial airlines can get you there just as well?

There's a great story about John Bogle, founder of the Vanguard Funds. He owned a lot of the stock in the holding company for his funds and was a stickler on expenses. But he didn't just talk about them. He led by example. He would take the bus to appointments rather than grab a taxi, saving a few extra dollars every time. The benefit from that frugal mentality was passed on to mutual fund shareholders in the form of very low fees. Even today, Vanguard Funds are worth considering as an investment, if the performance warrants, because they have the lowest fees in the industry.

You can find management and director ownership in *Value Line* or in the quote program at Yahoo!Finance by getting a quote on a stock, then clicking on the Major Holders link under Ownership. It will show you what officers and directors own how much stock as well as listing the institutional owners, the amount they hold, and what percentage each represents. Below that link is the Insider Transactions. Click on that and go to a page listing all the buys and sells by management and directors. Ideally, you'd like to see many more buys than sells.

But don't be concerned if you see some selling. The management and directors typically have been with a company a long time, investing in the company many years before it goes public. At times, they have to sell stock for taxes, to purchase a new home, buy a diamond ring or two, pay for divorce attorneys, etc. In other words, once in a while, they need to raise money, and their stock represents a large part of their wealth. You would have a real concern if all the management and directors were selling at the same time and in large quantities. Your obvious conclusion would be to sell as well, because if they don't believe in the future of the company and they're running it, then you have no reason to own the stock either.

This is another data point that should give comfort to Comfort Zone investors. You should be able to rest more soundly if the officers and directors of the company are heavily invested in your company. It means they're taking care to make sure the business grows, which in turn makes the stock go up.

More Data, More Comfort

I've used the above six data points as the essence of what great stocks have. Not every great stock will have all of them. Nor will a stock with each of them necessarily be great. There are many more ratios or numbers to consider before making an investment. But if you use these to start your search, you can eliminate a lot of stocks quickly (and easily by using your computer to find them). When you find stocks with great management, strong growth, a high ROE, a low PSR, high profitability as well as large insider stock ownership, you've got a stock that's well worth investigating to the fullest.

There are many good books on how to analyze a stock, such as Benjamin Graham's *The Intelligent Investor* or Peter Lynch's *Beating the Street* and *One Up on Wall Street*. There's also the classic *Common Stocks and Uncommon Profits* by Philip Fisher and updated by his son Ken. It's a good idea to read one or all of these books to get a strong understanding for what to look for in a stock. While it takes extra work, no one has ever claimed investing is easy. Plus you'll be a lot more comfortable with more knowledge.

My purpose in this chapter was to highlight some of the best attributes of great stocks so you can eliminate many without wasting time. Finding the stocks with these or most of these elements will put you well on your way to your Comfort Zone.

8

Bountiful Bonds

Gentlemen prefer bonds.

—*Andrew Mellon*

B onds can play a big part in putting you in your Comfort Zone. They pay you income in the form of interest payments, then return all your money when they mature, if the company that issued them doesn't go bankrupt. If you buy the right bonds, which I'll explain how to do in this chapter, that won't be one of your worries. You'll always get your money back.

Some bonds pay you interest and also go up in value, appreciating with the stock of the same company. These are convertible bonds. Some bonds don't pay any interest, but are much sought after. These are zero coupon bonds. Some bonds adjust with inflation so your purchasing power is kept intact. They're called inflation-adjusted bonds. I'll explain each of these bonds later in the chapter.

In short, bonds are fantastic except for one thing. They're not for you. That is, they're not meant for individuals. They're an institutional investment.

Bonds trade in round lots of $100,000. That's considered a minimum purchase for a bond trader on Wall Street. Sure you can buy them in sizes of less than $100,000, but those are odd lots. When you buy them, you pay more and when you sell them you get lower bids than for round lots. Dealers don't want odd-lot inventories. They can't sell them to institutions. But don't despair. You can and should still own bonds.

Bond Basics

Before I get into how to own bonds, you should know what they are. Bonds are promises to pay. (Bonds are also referred to as "debt," while stocks are referred to as "equity.") A company, or the government, takes your money and in return gives you a piece of paper called a bond. There is a promise to repay you whatever the "face" amount of the bond is. The face amount is whatever dollar amount is printed on the bond. It also states when you will receive the money. That's called the maturity date.

Most bonds pay interest every 6 months. Some pay every year. Others pay only at maturity such as Treasury bills or zero coupon bonds. There's a distinction in bondland that you should know: a bill is anything that matures in less than one year; a note is anything that matures between 1 year and 10 years; a bond matures in more than 10 years. Most bonds are between 10 and 20 years, but there are still some issued for 30 years. Those are rare.

Bonds are very sensitive to interest rates. (You see, once again, the value of understanding interest rates is important in investing.) The longer the bond maturity, the more the bond will move when interest rates go up or down. That's because bond prices have to adjust to current levels of rates. For example, if you buy a bond that matures in 15 years and pays 9% interest, the bond's market price will move down if interest rates go up. That's because new bonds being issued will carry a higher interest rate in order to attract investors.

Let's say you bought a 10-year note with a 9% coupon (the stated interest rate for a note or bond) a year ago and new ones pay 10%, a full point more in interest than yours. If you paid 100% (also known as "par" on the Street), then you can see that if new notes yield 10% and sell at par, your note will have to sell for less than 100% to have an equivalent yield of 10%. How much lower? About 8%. The price would be 92.31% of $1,000 per note (vs. the 100% you paid). That means if you were to try to sell your notes, you would receive $923.10 per $1,000 bond, if you could get a round lot bid for them. That's a loss of $76.90 per bond. If you owned 10 of the $1,000 bonds, you would lose $769.00.

When you consider that your $1,000 bond is paying you $90 a year (9% interest), if rates moved up much more than the 1 percentage point, your loss would exceed the one year's worth of interest that you would be paid. If rates move up by 2 percentage points, the value of your bond would be 85.47%, getting close to 2 years' worth of interest payments.

But keep in mind that these price fluctuations only matter if you're actually going to sell your bonds. If you own very safe bonds, such as ones issued by the U.S. government or AAA-rated companies, you can be assured that if you hold your bonds to maturity, you will get your money back, or $1,000 per bond, exactly what you paid if you bought them at par. But you will not get any more interest on your bond than the rate stated on it. Your interest payments won't adjust to new levels (up or down).

As mentioned earlier there is one bond that the U.S. Treasury issues called an inflation-adjusted bond or TIPS (Treasury Inflation Protected Securities). It will adjust the coupon paid to you based on the inflation rate of the economy as measured by the Consumer Price Index for All Urban Consumers (CPI-U). You can find out the details and buy these directly from the Treasury Department at http://www.publicdebt.treas.gov/gsr/gsrlist.htm.

These bonds can give you real comfort if you believe interest rates are going to move up dramatically. While the initial rates are lower than normal treasury bonds, if inflation were to roar back, these securities will adjust to pay you more than the initial yield.

Most investors don't bother with these bonds. They tend to buy straight bonds, no adjusting, just payments every 6 months, thank you very much. As I mentioned, this market is really for institutions, but you can still buy bonds.

A Word on Municipal Bonds

I don't like them. These are bonds issued by local and state authorities that are exempt from income taxes. Therefore, they look appealing to investors who want income without paying taxes. But the yields on these bonds are lower than corporate and government bonds because of the tax exemption.

While your after-tax yield is about the same when you buy a muni bond as compared to a corporate bond, your absolute income is lower because your interest payments are lower. And there's something called AMT or alternative minimum tax, a tax that goes after "unearned" income. If you have too much income from municipal bonds, you'll have to pay the AMT.

There's more to dislike about these bonds. Individual investors can really get ripped off if they try to sell them. The muni bond market is made up of mostly regional brokerage firms who issue municipal bonds and have limited capital. They can't afford to hold a lot of bonds because they don't have the capital to support that inventory. So they don't like to buy bonds. They much prefer to sell them. Therefore, they make bids you try to refuse but can't because many times no one else will even give you a price on the bonds. And if you're only selling small amounts such as $10,000 or less you'll get an even lower bid. I've seen too many clients get severely ripped off by dealers who are more than happy to sell these bonds but have no interest in buying them. If you really must buy a muni bond, only do it if you will absolutely, positively hold it until maturity, and you don't have a problem with AMT. And buy them only if you live in a high-tax area where the tax benefit outweighs the disadvantages. If you have to sell it before maturity, be prepared for a shock.

If you are determined to own muni bonds, then a muni bond fund is the way to go. There are funds that specialize in certain states as well as funds that buy munis from many different states.

Back to Bond Basics: Bond Ratings

I've given you some of the red flags about bonds. There are still plenty of good reasons to own them, mostly because of the steady income they send your way, unless there's a problem. Here's a way to avoid most problems.

Bonds are rated by four agencies: Standard & Poor's Corporation, Moody's Investors Service, Fitch Investors Service, and Duff and Phelps, Inc. Each uses a grading system to help investors determine the quality of a bond, or more exactly, the likelihood the bond will pay interest and principal at maturity. You want to focus on bonds that have the highest likelihood of making the payments.

On the grading scale, the highest rating from Standard & Poor's is AAA. The lowest is D. Moody's uses a little different scale: Aaa is the best and C is the lowest. Fitch uses AAA to D. Duff and Phelps uses a number system from 1 to 14, with 1 being the highest.

The real cutoff for investors interested in staying in their Comfort Zone is the difference between investment grade and noninvestment grade bonds. If you stay with investment grade bonds, you'll almost always be fine. However, a high rating is not a guarantee. Over a 15- or 20-year period things can change significantly for a company. Of course, problems don't usually happen overnight and a troubled company will be downgraded by the agencies if it does suffer a decline. When a bond goes from investment grade to noninvestment grade, the price for the bond goes way down. That's why you have to at least track the rating your bond receives as long as you own it.

The dividing line for Standard & Poor's between investment grade and noninvestment grade is BBB. If a bond goes below the BBB (say to a BB or B level), it will no longer be eligible for investment by most institutions. For Moody's, the break point is Baa. (Moody's has an excellent Web site explaining its ratings at: http://invest-faq.com/articles/bonds-moody-ratings.html) You want to buy bonds that are BBB or better (S&P designated), or Baa or better (Moody's rating). You'll find the most often quoted rating service is S&P, so I'll use that for the rest of this discussion.

I don't recommend BBB bonds for first time investors in bonds. You're too close to the edge. While their yields are more attractive than higher-rated issues, you can't feel too comfortable if you're wondering whether your bond will slip one more notch and go below investment grade. Once that happens, you get lower prices and questionable interest payments. Don't start your bond experience with BBB bonds.

That doesn't mean you have to buy AAA or U.S. Treasury issues to get totally comfortable. It means you want to stay in single A or better bonds. That way you know your income stream is safe. And since you're looking to hold your bonds until maturity, the price fluctuations from interest-rate changes won't affect your comfort level. You still have to monitor the credit rating on your bond. You can do that through the broker where you bought the bond. Brokerage firms can quickly tell you the rating on any bond.

The Famous Bond Ladder

Now the question becomes which is the best maturity to buy. You'll find that the longer the maturity date on the bond, the higher the interest rate, unless there's an inverted yield curve (when short rates are higher than long rates), which happens so rarely you won't likely see one. The rule of thumb is: The longer you hold the bond, the more interest you receive for your patience. (Once again, you can see the value of patience in investing.) This isn't because of your patience, though. It is an inflation and risk premium.

You may find in your initial investment quest that a 15-year bond has the highest yield. But you may not want to hold a bond for 15 years. You may be concerned about interest rates going higher. Remember what happens to bond prices when rates go up? It's not pretty. Even if you can hold the bond for 15 years, when rates rise, you'll want to own newer bonds because they will yield more. What if interest rates don't go higher, as you expect? What if they go lower? Then your bond will go up in price, but new bonds will have lower interest rates. The point here is not so much the price, because you've already seen why you want to hold it to maturity. Rather, the issue is that interest rates can go anywhere they damn well please and won't give you any warning as to when or where they're going. You want to approach bond buying like you don't know which way rates are going because, of course, you don't. No one does.

The way to be totally secure about buying bonds is to purchase what is called a ladder of bonds. Basically it means you buy a note that matures in 2 years, another note that matures in 5 years, a bond that matures in 10 years and maybe one that matures in 15 years or more. You may want to also own some 1 year or less bills if you know you'll need your money in that time frame.

If you picture the maturity dates (2, 5, 10, 15) as rungs on a ladder, you can see why this method is called the bond ladder. If you evenly distribute your money up the ladder, you will always have some money coming in within 2, 3 or 5 years to reinvest. That sounds great when rates are going higher. But if rates are going lower, you will reinvest in notes or bonds that will yield lower income than the note that is maturing. Which is why you've got those longer bonds bought at higher yields to help assuage that pain.

A bond ladder takes the stress out of guessing which way interest rates will go. You don't know. So invest accordingly. Sometimes you'll benefit from the ladder because rates will go higher, and you'll reinvest with better income. Sometimes you'll benefit from the ladder because rates are going lower, and your longer-term investments will continue to pay you at higher than current rates. As long as you don't have to sell any of your bonds, and they're all investment grade, the ladder works extremely well.

How Many Bonds to Buy?

This is really a three-part question: how many bonds to buy of any one maturity; how many bonds to buy for the initial position; and how many bonds in total to buy.

The number of bonds to buy for each maturity on your ladder (you can use 1 year, 3 years, 5 years, 7 years, and 10 years if you like; the actual maturities aren't as important as the spreading of them) should be an equal percentage for each rung. For example, if you choose to use 1 year, 3 years, 5 years, 10 years, and 15 years, then put 20% of your bond allocation in each maturity.

Don't try to get aggressive here and skew the holdings to the long end, even if you think rates are going lower. That's because rates have a way of doing things you don't expect. If 30-year U.S. Treasury bonds are paying 20%, you might guess correctly that rates will go down from there. (At one point, the 30-year U.S. Treasury paid 14% interest; 20% might happen, but the likelihood of this is almost zero because that rate would reflect an inflation problem that the Fed would do its very best to avoid.) Conversely, you may be convinced rates are going higher and have the temptation to put all your funds into the short end, looking to invest more when you determine rates are at their highest. Resist the temptation. Just put together a nice ladder and let interest rates do what they will. Again, you'll be much more in your Comfort Zone with a good multistep ladder than with one rung or two.

As for how much to buy in each maturity depends on how much you're going to allocate to bonds. How much you allocate to bonds has often been answered with how old you are. One simple method is to take your age as the percentage. If you're 30, put 30% in bonds. If you're 70, put 70%. For your own comfort, this isn't a bad rule of thumb. However, you may need more in bonds because it's your only source of income. Then you'll want to put more like 80% or 90% in them—but not 100%.

That's because you really owe it to yourself to own stocks. Stocks can appreciate and help you preserve your purchasing power. They also can pay nice dividends that often times are as good as or better than the income from bonds. But those dividends aren't as secure as interest payments. There's more risk to them. Buy the stocks for their capital appreciation potential and bonds will supply income.

Ways to Buy Bonds

Bonds are different from stocks in many ways. One of them has to do with the way they trade. Most bonds trade on a desk in a brokerage firm. There are a few that trade on the New York Stock Exchange but those are less than 5% of the total bond universe.

Those bond desks love to trade with institutions, not individuals. They price their bonds for institutions. Individuals are treated as nuisances. But you can still buy bonds from your broker. You can see most brokers' bond inventories online during the trading day if you use an online broker. Your stockbroker can get you bond offerings if you use a full-service broker.

The quote you receive will tell you the maturity of the bond, the price of the bond, and two yields: the current yield and the yield to maturity. The current yield is the one that takes the interest payment and divides it by the price you pay. If you buy a 6% bond at 90% of par, your yield is 6.67% (6/90). Since you're buying this bond at a discount to par (which is 100%), your yield to maturity will be higher than your current yield because the 10-point difference between where you buy it and the maturity value of 100 is added into your return. The yield to maturity for this bond would depend on when it comes due. If it's in one year, you'll have a very high yield to maturity because those 10 points will come within one year, just like an interest payment. If the bond matures in 10 years, it will be less than

1% because of the length of time it takes to collect the principal. Of course, the yield to maturity changes as interest rates change because the future value of that payment will go up or down, depending on the interest rate used to calculate the present value.

Lots of gibberish, I know, but stuff you should be aware of. You don't have to really know all this but if you understand the idea, you'll be better off. The idea being that there are two yields to your bond: the current yield, which is what you live on, as it were, and the yield to maturity, which is the total yield of the bond that incorporates the added principal you receive on a bond, if you buy it below par, once it matures.

The best way to buy a bond is to know exactly what grade of bond you want and what maturity. That helps define your universe quickly. Without doing a great deal of due diligence, you can be fairly comfortable that any bond rated AA or better will make its payments, whether you've ever heard of the company or not. Initially, I'd recommend you do some research by looking at an online broker's inventory or by having your broker send you an e-mail of bonds the firm offers.

Most brokers list their bonds by maturity date, ones closest to maturity are first and then they go out the yield curve, which is a curve that plots yields according to their maturities. You'll see the name of the issuing company; the coupon, which is what the interest payment will be; and the rating of the bond. There will also be the price you pay, the current yield, and the yield to maturity. You buy bonds in increments of $1,000. If you see an ExxonMobil bond on your broker's list with a coupon of 6%, maturing in 5 years, that means you'll be paid $60 a year for 5 years for every $1,000 of the bond you buy. Your payments would be $30 every 6 months for each bond you buy until the bond matures.

Each day the bond inventory changes. By studying a few days' worth of bond lists, you will quickly get comfortable with what's on them and how to read them. When you finally get ready to buy, you simply put in your order online or through your broker. If you liked the ExxonMobil bond described above, and you want to allocate 20% of your total bond money to that purchase, you can bid for the bond by putting in a price that is a little below the offering price or you can simply pay the price listed. It never hurts to try to buy it a little cheaper. Sometimes the trader will be glad to get rid of it and will hit your bid. Other times, you won't be so lucky.

Now, THIS IS IMPORTANT: Be sure you are comfortable with owning the bond because you're not going to sell it. Remember that, especially if you're only buying $3,000 worth or some relatively small amount (at least, for Bondland). That's because the bid you get for small amounts of bonds does not resemble the price you pay for them. Buy bonds to hold, not to trade or sell later.

Structuring your ladder with five different bonds is the best way to insure diversified risk. You'll be tempted to buy more of one company because its yields will be higher but resist the temptation. When there is too much discrepancy between one company and another in the same rating (such as AA or A), most likely that issuer has been put on credit watch by the agencies and is in danger of having its debt downgraded. So pick five different companies with five different maturities and relax. You'll be in your Comfort Zone immediately.

Bond Funds

You can also buy bonds through mutual funds. There are so many mutual fund types that you can build mutual fund bond ladders if you like. The big advantage with mutual funds is that you get strong diversification in the portfolio and professional management. Of course, you pay a fee for those attributes; but if you are not comfortable with buying and watching your bonds, then use a bond fund.

But watch out for the bond funds that specialize in longer maturities, ones that buy bonds with average maturities over ten years. That's because you have principal at risk when rates go up. If you use a bond fund for your longer-term "rung" on your ladder, make sure you understand that you may not get all of your principal back, especially if you buy it and then rates continue to move up over the next several years. If you have to sell that fund, you will not get all your principal back because the value of the fund will be down from where you bought it simply because the value of the bonds it holds are lower. There's no way around this fact. That's why using bond funds with maturities of less than five years is the best way to go. It keeps price fluctuations smaller.

You can find very good information on bond funds at several of the fund sites. A few of them are www.vanguard.com or www.fidelity.com.

There's also a great site for general bond funds and how to use them at www.investopedia.com. I highly recommend it for understanding bond funds more fully.

Other Types of Bonds

I mentioned a couple of other bonds in the opening of this chapter. One of them referred to a bond that doesn't pay any interest. That's a zero coupon bond. It won't pay you interest but you buy it at a discount to par (less than 100%), and at maturity you get 100% of the face value of the bond. In other words, you might buy one at 60% of par that matures in 10 years. Then in 10 years, you'll get 100% of the face value of the bond. In this example, you would pay $600 for every $1,000 worth of bonds you buy. After ten years, you receive $1,000 dollars, or income of $400.

There are two catches to these bonds. The first is obvious. You don't get any money until you cash in the bond. The second is that you have to pay income taxes on the inferred income that you're not receiving. That's right. You owe money on money you don't get until much later. How that works is that every year, the value of the bond increases, approaching $1,000. After one year of holding it, the bond may be worth $650. Or may be worth $550 if interest rates go up. But as far as the IRS is concerned, there are taxes to be paid, based on the imputed value of the bond as it approaches maturity. This is called the original issue discount, the difference between par and what you paid for the bond. Every year you pay taxes on a portion of that discount. Of course, if you buy zero coupon bonds in your IRA, the tax consideration isn't of consequence. So there may be a place for them in your overall investing strategy, but you'll want to learn more about them. A good source is www.sec.gov/answers/zero.htm

Another interesting bond is not exactly a bond. It's a combination of a stock and a bond called a convertible bond. The convertible bond has a coupon, much lower than a straight corporate bond, but it also has one great feature. It can be converted into stock at anytime the holder wishes. I only want to introduce this type of bond to you so you can use it as a defensive investment if you feel the need. These are, like corporate bonds, really for institutional investors. The way you want to own them is in a mutual fund that specializes in them. You can find a list of these funds in Morningstar or in the mutual fund screening programs at Yahoo!Finance or Marketwatch or on AOL. They can be very rewarding but also very tricky and are best left to professionals. You can learn much more about convertible bonds at www.mutualfunds-info.com/bondconvertiblefundsindexmutual.

A word on preferred stock. It's a cross between equity and debt. But it is neither equity nor debt. It is a class of stock that usually pays a dividend, but that dividend is not secured or guaranteed, the way a bond coupon payment is. And preferred stock does not participate in the appreciation of a company unless it is a convertible preferred, a security that converts into the common stock.

You may hear about the higher yields that straight preferred stocks carry. That's because there's more risk with them. A preferred stock is definitely, totally, an institutional market. There's even a tax advantage for corporations to buy them. Don't even think about investing in preferred stocks unless you have thoroughly investigated them, have a broker that specializes in them, and understand that you are the ant playing in the elephants' path. They don't trade very much. Information on individual issues is almost impossible to find. They can be called away from you just when you want to keep them. They can go way down in price but not way up. Trust me. Don't bother with preferred stocks. They will drag you out of your Comfort Zone kicking and screaming. I don't even want to give you a reference for investigating them further because they're just not for you. I'm reluctant to recommend mutual funds that specialize in them. That's how much you shouldn't be involved with them.

Once Again, Stick to the Basics

I want to reemphasize the comfort of sticking to the basics. You don't need complicated bonds to receive a good income from them. You want to buy straightforward, investment-grade corporate or government bonds. The government bonds you can buy without a broker at www.sec.gov. You save a commission and can roll over your funds online at maturity. You can also buy bond funds directly from the mutual funds, either online or through the mail. To find the right bond funds, use the mutual fund screening programs that are on the same sites as the stock screening programs already listed.

Bonds will take you a long way into your Comfort Zone as long as you don't try to reach too far for yield. Remember that the lowest risk is with government bills and everything else is measured against those. The further you get from government bills, notes, and bonds, in terms of yield for comparable maturities, the more risk you are taking. More risk means less comfort.

9

New Industry, New Company, New Markets

Just think if you'd been down there at Kitty Hawk and you'd seen this guy go up, and all of a sudden this vision hits you that tens of millions of people would be doing this all over the world someday. It would bring us closer together and everything. You'd think, my God, this is something to be in on. Despite putting in billions and billions and billions of dollars, the net return to owners of the entire airline industry, if you'd owned it all, and you'd put up all this money, is less than zero.

—Warren Buffett

Every investor gets excited when a new industry seems to be forming. I use the word "seems" because many industries look great in the early stages, only to disappear before they develop, simply because there was no market for the product or the cost was too dear for the consumer or end user. There are always new products, companies, and industries being created. Many of them go on to be wonderfully successful. You, as an investor, want to know what they are, how to invest in them, and remain comfortably in your Comfort Zone.

Some examples of companies that revolutionized an industry are Microsoft, Yahoo!, Amazon, eBay, Google, Apple, Southwest Airlines, Schwab, IBM, America Online. Similarly, there are new markets that develop, such as Japan did after the war. China currently is showing strong capitalist tendencies with billions of people soon to become important consumers. India is emerging as an economic powerhouse as well.

Read and Heed!

So how do you, as an investor, find these great opportunities and then invest in them? Before I go into that, remember the stock Iridium I described in chapter 1? It's a great example of what happens when a new idea doesn't work. Keep it in mind whenever you read about or hear of a great, new, can't-miss investment.

So the million-dollar question is: How do you buy the companies that are going to be roaring successes and avoid the ones like Iridium? No one knows. If they did, they wouldn't tell you because they wouldn't want their secret to get out. But you can still participate in winning stocks. You just won't know until well into their successes that you've made the right choice.

The Secret

The secret to buying winning stocks in new industries or new ideas is simple: The answer lies in buying a small amount of many of them. By definition, each stock is an unknown, and the future for it is fraught with peril. That's true for any stock because each company has to prove its worth in the marketplace. When you see a new idea or a new company, you can do your research and buy a small amount of shares, if it meets certain criteria which I'll give later.

Many readers may say, "Wow. A small amount of shares. That's not going to make me rich." They're wrong. A stock that does very well will go up, split, and continue to go up. One small stock I bought for my children went from $8 to $113 in a couple of years. That's $800 into $11,300. That was almost one year in college, at that time, from an $800 investment. There are many stories like this. Along with those I have to add that I've bought some that went from $50 to $5. But because my portfolios were always balanced, I kept in the Comfort Zone, those losses were not large enough to damage the overall performance.

So the first way to invest in new ideas is to buy small amounts, even 10 shares will do of many companies. I should add right away that these types of investments should be only a small part of your overall portfolio, no more than 10%. They should be made only after you've developed your Core Holdings portfolio.

New Company Evolution

Before I go any further with more ways to invest in these new opportunities, you should be aware of how new companies evolve. That way you have a better chance of picking winners. Most new companies start with an idea and no money, unless they're the brainchild of Bill Gates, or someone already wealthy. Even then, however, the founders won't risk all of their money on one idea. Sometimes they do, but those are usually companies that don't make it, and the founders are people you've never heard of—because they're poor now.

Most new companies make it on OPM, Other People's Money. The first "other people" to get tapped are friends and families of the founders. And boy do they get tapped! Over and over until the relatives and friends won't take phone calls any more. When that well runs dry and the new product or service still isn't on the market or is generating very little revenues, the founder goes to the venture capital community, where he realizes that his excitement is not shared by the world. In fact, he learns that no one believes he can make it work.

But if it does, it certainly won't be as profitable as he thinks it will be. At least, this is what every venture capitalist will tell the founder. That way, when the founder finally has reached the starvation level and doesn't have any options left, he will accept the low valuation the venture capitalists put on the company. Instead of being valued at, say, the $10 a share the founder wants, the venture capitalist offers 10 cents a share. After much crying, begging, and negotiating, the founder usually takes 15 cents, feels violated, and then proceeds with enough money to actually get his product or service to the market.

The thing for you as an investor to get from this so far is not that all venture capitalists are mean and evil, because clearly not *all* are. But not all venture capitalists are created equal. A company backed by a well-known venture firm such as Kleiner, Perkins will have more of an appeal to investors than one backed by Smith and Smith, which is doing its very first deal. For a list of venture capital firms and links to their Web sites where you can learn more about them, see www.nvca.org. It's the site for the National Venture Capital Association.

So when you're looking at new opportunities, look for the backers behind the company. You can find that in the prospectus of a new issue or in the SEC Web site (www.edgar.gov) that shows all of the filed reports of a public company.

Let's say that our hypothetical company has gotten funded, worked hard, and is bringing in revenues. Now it needs more money to expand. So management decides to go public. That is, they will sell stock to the public for the first time, known as an IPO or initial public offering. The venture capitalists are as excited as the management, maybe more so, since their 15-cent stock is now worth $10 or more. When the IPO is announced, this is your first chance, as a public investor, to be involved directly with the stock. But it isn't the first opportunity you have to be involved with the company.

Public Companies That Invest in Private Ones

That's because you can invest in stocks that invest your money in venture capital deals. There aren't many of them but a few are:

American Capital Strategies (ACAS-NASDAQ) has three main areas of business: as a financial partner in management and employee buyouts; as a provider of senior debt, mezzanine, and equity financing for buyouts led by private equity firms; and as a provider of capital directly to private and small public companies. ACAS generally invests up to $150 million in each transaction; and as of this writing since its IPO in 1997, it has invested about $5 billion in companies in services, transportation, construction, wholesale, retail, health care and industrial, consumer, chemical, and food products.

Allied Capital (ALD-NYSE) is a public investment firm specializing in growth capital investments, recapitalizations, acquisitions, buyouts, note purchases, and bridge financing. It typically makes mezzanine and equity investments in middle-market companies, noninvestment grade tranches of commercial mortgage-backed securities, and collateralized debt obligations. The firm seeks to invest in the following sectors: business services, financial services, consumer products, health-care services, industrial products, retail, energy services, and broadcasting.

Capital Southwest (CSWC-NASDAQ) is a venture capital investment firm with an objective to achieve capital appreciation through long-term investments in businesses believed to have favorable growth potential. The company's investments are focused on early stage financings, expansion financings, management buyouts, and recapitalizations in a broad range of industry segments. The portfolio is a composite of companies in which CSWC has major interests as well as a number of developing companies and marketable securities of established publicly owned companies.

There are more of these types of stocks. You can find them by using Yahoo!Finance (www.finance.yahoo.com). Just enter the symbol of any of the above three, click on Go. When the quote page appears, look on the left side of the page. Click on Competitors. There will be four or five other stocks listed.

I do not recommend any of these because by the time you read this, much will have changed. Maybe new management. Maybe some bad investments. Maybe the valuations are way too high. Rather, I am letting you know that there are ways to invest in new companies or new industries without having to do it directly or singularly. These stocks and their competitors give you a chance to participate in private deals as well as great diversification. Look up each of these stocks. Look at their numbers. Get some research on them, which you can also find on the Yahoo!Finance site. These stocks, like all stocks and mutual funds mentioned in this book, are for example purposes only. Too much time will elapse between my writing this and you reading it for specific stocks to be recommended.

Participating in New Markets

By this I mean new consumer markets such as China. How do you, as an individual, get involved in the Chinese market? A couple of ways.

First, you find companies that are already doing business there, either because of existing, in-country manufacturing or American companies exporting to China. Good examples are GE, Boeing, GM, Starbucks, Potash (agricultural fertilizer), UTStarcom Inc. (a cell phone company), Intel, and eBay. While most of these are large companies with sales in many countries, the percentage that China represents will most likely grow. One, UT-Starcom, which is still relatively small, has most of its revenues coming from China and India.

There aren't any reports or screens that tell you what companies are doing business in China or other new markets. You have to find these by reading about each company. One of the best sources is a company's Web site.

Always remember there are mutual funds that specialize in one country or in a region. There are plenty of Asia/Pacific funds that invest in China as well as funds that only focus on China.

Investing in New Markets

You now have the tools to invest in new markets, whether they're new products or services or new countries or regions. You can buy specific stocks that do the work for you, getting professional management as well as diversification. Or you can buy mutual funds that focus on smaller growth companies as well as funds that specialize in certain countries or regions of the world.

By staying away from individual stocks that may or may not make it through the extremely difficult start-up years, you can still participate in this highly rewarding part of the investment world by using these other, more comfortable sources. And if you keep this part of your portfolio at less than 10%, you'll always be in your Comfort Zone.

PART FOUR

HOW TO INVEST

10

Exploit Your Computer: It's Your Money Machine

The market, like the Lord, helps those who help themselves.

—Warren Buffett

We, as investors, are very fortunate to live in the age of the computer. What used to take hours of research can now be done in seconds, displayed, analyzed, and acted upon in minutes. Not that you want to buy your investments only a few minutes after discovering them. But you can eliminate a lot of unwanted stuff in a hurry.

While the computer is a great tool, it is only a tool. If it could pick only the best stocks or run programs that traded stocks profitably, then the brightest programmers would have the most money, which they don't (Bill Gates being the exception that proves the rule!). Remember that your computer is like a robot: It can only serve you. It can't make decisions. You have to do that. And if you want to stay in your Comfort Zone, then using your computer wisely will serve you well. And if you don't have a computer, I highly recommend you buy one.

What Your Computer Can't Do

Let's start with realistic expectations. The computer can do a lot of things, but it can't do everything.

It can't pick a winning stock every time

In other words, you can't write a program that will guarantee a winning stock. No one can. That's because stocks are not just numbers. They represent companies run by human beings. What investors experienced with Enron, MCI, and Tyco when they fell apart due to the dishonesty of management is a reminder that bad things happen to good companies. No computer can catch those criminals. And it's not just criminal behavior. It's changes in interest rates, monster storms knocking out power plants, or any number of disasters that can't be predicted. Just because your computer delivers a list of "winners" from a program, doesn't mean you can blindly buy them. You need to look deeper than that.

It can't predict the future any better than a fortune teller can

It can take a lot of factors and make good guesses, but again, it can't know the future. That's especially true for trading programs that suggest, sometimes almost promise, that if used, you'll be able to trade stocks or currencies or futures with such success that in only days you'll retire. Computers can't do that no matter what program you buy.

It can't give you the best information for free

The best data banks cost money. They are updated continuously. Data are analyzed. That takes people—which costs money. While many of the free sites are great, they will not have the depth of sites that charge for their services or the analysis of the data.

For example, *Investor's Business Daily* is a great newspaper that runs a site at www.investors.com. It's the newspaper put onto the Web. It costs, as of this writing, $235 a year. The information jammed into the site is unique

and extremely useful. The newspaper takes large amounts of data and analyzes them according to a proprietary system that ranks stock in various
ways. It gives the top volume percentage leader, the top percentage price
gainer, relative ratios, and much more. You can't find many of these anywhere else on the Web. While it's not absolutely necessary for success to
have access to this analysis, it does make your research easier and faster
when you use this site. (I'll give a number of sites to consider later in the
chapter.)

What Your Computer Can Do

Your computer can keep you informed. Many companies will send you an
e-mail when they have a press release or make the news. You simply go to
their Web site, register with them, and when the company makes an announcement or files a form with the Securities and Exchange Commission
(SEC), you will know about it. It shows up in your e-mail inbox.

The SEC filings are often 8-Ks. An 8-K is required by the SEC whenever
there is anything material that has happened in the company, such as an
officer or director having a change in compensation or a new company being bought. You can view all of these filings at one of the most potent and
important sites for investors: The SEC Web site at www.sec.gov. While it
takes a little time to figure out all the various forms, here's a short list of the
important ones:

- **Form 10-Q.** The quarterly report that companies are required
  to file with the SEC, but are no longer required to send to shareholders.

- **Form 10-K.** The annual report that you will receive as in investor
  in a company, but if you want to read it when it's filed, it's on the
  SEC site.

- **Form 8-K.** Any material change at the company must be filed with
  the SEC. With the new regulations under the Full Disclosure Act
  (Reg FD for Regulation Full Disclosure), almost everything is now
  considered material. If you have the e-mail notification service from

a company you own or follow, you can get this information the same time the press picks it up.

- **Form 4.** States changes in ownership of stock for directors and officers. This form can help you see if your company is issuing a lot of options or stock grants that dilute your ownership in the company, as well as to see the buys and sells of management and directors.

More Computer Competence

The computer can track all of your holdings, keeping a record of when you bought your stock, how much you paid, how much you made or lost when you sold it. It's a great tool when it comes time for income taxes. You don't have to keep all your records on paper anymore. Just enter your buys and sells into a program and let the computer do the rest. They'll save you hours each year. Some of them are free.

Your computer can find answers. One of the most powerful sites for answers is www.ask.com. Simply put your request in the form of a question, and within seconds, you'll have a list of Web sites with the answer or close to the answer you're seeking. For example, if you wanted to know what 30 stocks are in the Dow Jones Industrial Average, you ask: What stocks are in the Dow Jones Industrial Average? It's really that easy.

Your computer can communicate with a company. Most companies have Investor Relations departments. Their job is to get information to shareholders or potential shareholders as well as communicate with them. If you go to a company's Web site, it will have a tab labeled Contact Us. Clicking on that tab will usually generate an e-mail box that allows you to send a question directly to the IR department. If there is no e-mail contact, it will give the address and/or the phone number. If you call the company, ask for the Investor Relations Department to get answers. Don't ask for the president. In some of the smaller companies, the president is the IR Department, but start by asking for the IR Department. If you don't like the answers you get from them, then ask for the president.

Your computer can help you vent. If you own a stock that keeps going lower or hasn't moved in years and YOU JUST CAN'T TAKE IT ANY MORE, then you might like to go to a message board and vent, along with all other shareholders who feel the same way. Message boards are kept on several large Web sites such as America Online or Yahoo!Finance. By entering the symbol of your stock, you go to a quote page that has a link to the message board devoted exclusively to your stock. You can read what others have to say, but you can also add your comments as well as vent your frustration. Remember: Not everything you read on a message board is true. Some writers have hidden agendas. I discuss message boards and chat rooms more on page 159. Of course, you can always write the company and vent directly.

Web Sites to Use

There are a large number of Web sites and plenty of software programs that hype themselves as having great information. Some of them do. Many of them don't. The most important ones to avoid are the ones that focus on trading stocks or currencies or futures. They're not for you. Nothing takes you further from your Comfort Zone than trading. Besides, the game is so stacked against you, as an individual, that you *will* lose money. Avoid the trading sites and software.

Here are useful sites with investing information or programs that help you invest better or track your investments:

- **The Online Investor www.theonlineinvestor.com** On AOL, keyword: oli. This is a site run by me and my partner, James Hale. It's full of data and information such as stock splits, analyst recommendations, economic news, investor tips, top-ten dividend paying stocks by industry, specific stock analysis, and many other resources that will help you make better investment choices. Highly Recommended. (Yes, I run it, but I truly believe it's a helpful site—and hundreds of thousands of readers agree!)

- **The Wall Street Journal Online http://online.wsj.com/home/us** This is the famous newspaper without the back section where the stock prices are. You can find stock prices all over the Web, but the text of the paper is extremely helpful to investors who want to learn more about companies, the latest business news, as well as how to invest better. Highly Recommended. Has a $79-a-year subscription fee; it costs less if you also buy the print edition.

- **Value Line www.valueline.com** I can't recommend this too highly. There is great comfort in the data and analysis that Value Line provides on 1,700 stocks, both large and mid caps. You can use it free at your local library. You can subscribe to it for $598 a year and have the print version delivered by mail weekly. Or you can subscribe online for $598 a year, which includes analytic tools that help you screen for stocks that fit your criteria for investing. Both the site and the print version explain clearly and in depth how to use the material. Full of stock recommendations and unique data. Very highly recommended.

- **Yahoo!Finance http://finance.yahoo.com** This great site contains lots of data, but be aware that it's not updated daily. Some of the data can be weeks or months old. However, it has links to many worthwhile databanks such as insider buying and selling, analyst recommendations on stocks, and dividend information such as the ex-dividend date, amount of the dividend, pay date (these are surprisingly hard to find on other sites or not available). The best way to use it is to explore all the links. There's plenty of research and analysis. Highly recommended.

- **MarketWatch www.marketwatch.com** This site offers business and economic news and so much more. Much like Yahoo!Finance, there are plenty of resources to help you find stocks and mutual funds. The front page is kept current throughout the day with breaking news while the links on the left go to industry-specific information. At the top of the page are tabs that give you access to Personal Finance with articles on investing; My Portfolios, a tracking page for all your stocks and any stocks you want to follow; Newsletters and Research—most of the newsletters are by subscription but there is commentary from some of them for free; and Investor Tools, a great way to keep up on the market. On the site, you can sign up for e-mail alerts on specific companies or have the news sent to your mobile phone and also track your portfolio. There's a customizable portfolio setup that lets you watch the data that are important to you as well as live quotes. All of these services require

that you sign up with Marketwatch, giving them your e-mail address so they can send you stuff, but it's a small price to pay for the
information. There are also premium services in the Investor Tools
site which cost money. The final free tab at the top of the page is
TV/Radio. Business interviews from TV or radio are stored on this
page. It is an excellent site and is highly recommended.

- **MSN Money www.msnmoney.com** This is a site that directs you
to mostly paying sites, as in not free, that will help you with investing. For example, if you click on Stocks, there appears a list of brokerage firms such as Schwab, Ameritrade, Sharebuilder, Nasdaq,
and many more. Though no direct information is given, it is a good
resource for finding other sites. Recommended.

- **MSN Money Central www.moneycentral.msn.com** Different site
but still part of MSN Money. If you follow business news on CNBC,
this is where they have their interviews and information available.
There are many of the standard investing features already described,
but there are extras such as the Tax section, Banking and Planning
links that help you with taxes, retirement planning, insurance, college, and others. Updated news continuously. This is a great site
with plenty of help for investors. Highly recommended.

- **AOL Personal Finance www.aol.com** Or AOL keyword: pf.
Loaded with information about investing, this site has portfolio services that allow you to track stocks, showing profits and losses, and
has large database access through Thomson Financial and Hoover's.
Highly recommended.

Other Sites Worth Visiting

- **Hoover's www.hoovers.com** Contains a lot of data and information on stocks. Used as a primary resource for many other Web
sites. There's a fee for this one. Recommended.

- **Thomson Financial Group www.thomsonfinancial.com** This
great site has data on over 45,000 stocks around the world, compiling

research from many different brokerage firms for stock information. Be prepared to pay, but it's well worth it if you use all its offerings. Highly recommended.

- **Briefing.com www.briefing.com** Get the Gold Package if you make the commitment. Designed for the long-term investor rather than the trader (it's $9.95 a month as of this writing), it has lots of great information, including calendars of upcoming IPOs, economic releases, earnings releases, etc. Highly recommended.

- **Morningstar.com www.morningstar.com** This a site has great information on stocks and mutual funds. Morningstar began as a resource for analyzing mutual funds, and is still the best in the business at that. Recently, it added stock information to its coverage of mutual funds. You have to pay, but it's definitely worth the cost. Highly recommended.

- **The Motley Fool www.fool.com** Most of the Fool's info is free, but it also has newsletter subscriptions that offer stock picks. There are plenty of message boards and chat rooms on this site as well as columns about investing. It takes a solid, long-term approach to investing but delivers its message in a way that millions like (not me, however). Recommended.

Software for Tracking Your Investments

- **Intuit Quicken www.quicken.intuit.com** As of this writing there are four choices for the software. The one you want is Premier Home. It's $69.99 and is a powerful package for tracking stocks, expenses, and taxes. It has these features: See where your money goes (never pretty, but very helpful when you do); create and manage a budget; monitor and pay bills on schedule; download data from your brokerage firm or bank (excellent part of the program that lets you analyze and work with the numbers); track your savings plan; maximize your investments (helps you see how each of your stocks, bonds, savings are doing and how to allocate your money for best results); find hidden tax deductions (based on your input, the program can identify which expenses go where); manage business and personal finance (tracking program for your stocks and other investments); create and track business invoices (can also be used for personal bills). Excellent program.

- **Microsoft Excel www.microsoft.com** This program takes a while to master but once done, you can track and manage your investments in any way you'd like. You have to input all the data, but you can then arrange it as you like, calculate returns automatically, and show profits and losses of each investment. It's a powerful tool but demands more time than most because it is not specifically written for investing. More for the moderate to advanced computer user than the novice. Excellent overall data program.

- **Microsoft Money www.microsoft.com/money/** As of this writing costs $79.95 for the Premium edition. Very slick program. With one password you can see what's in your checking account, your 401(k), your savings, and your investment account. It automatically updates these numbers so you don't have to go to each institution to see where you stand financially. It has most of the features of Intuit Quicken and a few more, such as online bill payment and graphics that show where your money is, and where it goes. Easy to use and understand. Highly recommended.

- **MoneyDance www.moneydance.com** Very easy to use. Though not quite as sophisticated as Microsoft Money or Quicken, it has enough features for most investors. It uses lots of graphics, showing what percentage each expenditure represents and much more; has an online bill pay feature; helps you create and follow a budget and shows you where you're straying; and brings your investments into focus with support for tracking stocks, bonds, CDs, mutual funds, etc. Security details show the performance of stocks and mutual funds over time. Stock splits and cost basis, important at tax time, are easy, and stock and mutual fund prices can be downloaded automatically. This is a good program for new investors. Compare it with MSN Money and Quicken before you buy since it may not have all the features you want. Highly recommended.

A Few More Words on Web Sites and Software

Some readers will wonder why I didn't include their favorite site or financial software. It's because new ones come and go all the time. The ones described here have been around for a while, offer great features for free or modest prices. Also, once you visit these sites, you'll see that there is very little differentiating one from another. Each will have some unique data or information or features, but there is a lot of duplication. Once you try all of them, you'll find a comfort level with one or two and then bookmark those for constant use.

You're looking for the most data you can find on a stock when you go to the Web sites. Many of them will have portfolio trackers that will help with your income taxes. But I would recommend you get a separate software program that allows you to input or download your specific trades so you control that data. You don't want to depend on an outside source for your tax information.

One other great resource for software and/or research might be your brokerage firm. If you're using one of the large online brokers such as Scottrade, Schwab, Ameritrade, E-Trade, or others, you'll find a number of programs that help you analyze stocks, give stock research, offer portfolio analysis and tracking, and many more services.

As an example, at Scottrade (www.scottrade.com), where online commissions are $7 a trade, no matter how many shares you trade, you get the following features in the most basic account: a personalized Quote list (that means you enter the symbols you want to track and they are automatically updated with new prices on each trade), Live Stock Ticker (you can watch trades on stocks as they occur), Streaming Intraday, Daily and Weekly Charts (updated charts of stock prices in real time), Stock Market Research, Dow Jones Real Time News for Investors, Top Ten Lists (stocks that have reached new highs for the year, stocks with the most volume, and stocks with the highest percentage gains and losses), and much more helpful information.

Each of the online firms is trying to offer you the most for your commissions. They all represent incredible value, given the low cost of placing stock orders. But they don't hold your hand or recommend specific stocks. Some of them have partnered with large firms for their research, such as Schwab with Goldman Sachs and Standard & Poor's, so you can also find research on many of their sites. But you'll have to input the stock symbol and see what research is available for that specific stock. None of the online brokers will actually recommend a stock to you. You have to find your own stocks, then see what the online broker or its research affiliates think of it.

I'll discuss online brokers in more detail in chapter 13.

About Message Boards and Chat Rooms

Message boards, as mentioned above, are on most of the larger Web sites where there are stock quotes. There's usually a link to the board or room once you've gotten a quote on a stock. When you go to the board, which is a Web site page, you'll see a list of headlines. Click on one of them, and you'll see a message from a writer.

Be aware that message boards are anonymous. There are no regulators checking on truthfulness. Anyone can say anything, true or false. So don't believe everything you read on the boards. That doesn't mean you should avoid them.

What I have found is that message boards about a specific stock usually have one or two dedicated investors who really know the stock. I'm thinking now of a couple of biotech stocks I own. At least one of the writers is a doctor, another is a researcher, and they write the most erudite messages about the science of the company. I learn a great deal about applications and the potential for new discoveries. I'm not a scientist by any means, and these two writers have helped me understand this stock better than I ever could on my own. So there is value in those posts.

However, they only write positive messages because they both own the stock. Many of the message writers will state next to their names if they own the stock or are shorting the stock (means they want it to go down). You have to read every post with an understanding of the position the writer has. If they're long (they own it), naturally they'll focus on the positive attributes of the stock. If they're short the stock, they'll keep emphasizing the negative. Read each one with the hope of understanding a stock better, a stock you've already chosen to follow and know something about. Don't go to a message board and look for unbiased opinions. That's not their purpose. They're a forum for stockholders to interact with one another and extol the virtues or vices of a stock.

Chat rooms aren't as popular any more. But the same caveats apply to them as to the message boards. Most of the participants will not be there to learn but to convince other members in the room to sell or buy the stock. Again, there may be some good information related in these rooms so don't dismiss them. Just be very wary of believing anything you read.

11

Day Trading
Is for Dummies

My favorite holding period is forever.

—*Warren Buffett*

Trading is the siren song of Wall Street. It seems like it would be easy to make money from all those little symbols streaming across a ticker tape, the prices of stocks going up and down. Surely, there's some method that can make you rich in all that movement. Trust me on this one thing: there isn't.

Trading is a loser's game. You will not make money from it, and I'll explain why. But you'll likely do it anyway, so later I'll give some ways to help bring the odds a little more in your favor, even though it still isn't enough to make money.

The Real Facts About Trading Stocks

Trading stocks is best left to the professionals. Don't try this at home. You can't do it. Just as professional ice skaters make their sport look so easy and graceful, pro traders have spent years perfecting their skills. And like skaters, you don't see any old ones. That's because stock trading takes its toll on your body, your nerves, and your mind. If you ever visit a trading desk of a brokerage firm, you'll see a bottle of pink liquid on many of the desks or in the drawers. That's because traders' stomachs are very, very upset most of the time.

Trading is the act of trying to tell the future movement of a stock in a very short period of time. Traders buy a stock in the hope it will go up a small amount so they can sell it at a profit. Of course, they don't buy just 100 shares. They're looking to pick up tens of thousands of shares, watch the stock move up a quarter to a half a point and then sell it, hopefully within minutes. Traders that can do that more than 50% of the time make a lot of money.

These pros have several things in their favor. They don't pay commissions on their trades so they save money when they buy and sell, and they are using the firm's capital, not their own. You, on the other hand, pay commissions and are playing with your own money. They also have the best information money can buy. They pay tens of thousands dollars a month for news sources and quote programs that will give them a split-second advantage over the competition. You don't have any of these things.

Commissions play a big role in trading. Every time you buy or sell a stock, you pay a commission. Even if they're as low as $7 a trade, regardless of the number of shares, commissions add up quickly.

There's also the tax aspects of trading. Let's say you're lucky enough to make money at trading. You have to pay short-term taxes, which are the same as your income tax rate, rather than long-term capital gains. So you're paying higher taxes and lots of commissions, both taking chunks out of your gains.

As for information sources, even with your computer, unless you're willing to spend at least $5,000 to $10,000 a month for a professional data and information service like Bloomberg, real time quotes, charting services, and other news services, you won't be able to keep up with the pros, your competition.

Then there's the "wash rule." If you take a loss in a stock and want to use that loss in your taxes (which all sane people do), you can't buy the stock again for 30 days. Keeping careful track of your gains and losses is essential if you're trading and don't want to violate this rule.

Trading takes constant vigilance if you're doing it right. You can't buy or sell a stock, then go do your job, come back, and hope for the best. You need to monitor every up and down tick, and get out of your position quickly, either to capture a gain or minimize a loss. In other words, if you have a day job and are trying to trade, you have to understand you are playing the game against people for whom trading *is* their day job. Stocks can move quickly, and if you're going to preserve your capital, you need to get out of a losing position fast. If you're not watching every trade of your stocks, you can't do that.

The Comfort of Investing

Investing means you don't have to be glued to a computer every second of the day. It means you don't have to think about taxes or commissions. By the way, one rule of investing is that you never let taxes determine a buy or sell decision. In other words, if you have a large gain in a stock and have determined it should be sold and still have one month to go before you qualify for capital gains taxes, you sell it today. You don't wait for a month because anything can happen in a month and often does. Letting taxes rule your investing decisions is a sure way to diminish your success. Besides, paying taxes is the American way of knowing you've been a profitable investor.

Investing is all about the long term, the longer the better. As the quote opening this chapter suggests, there's nothing wrong with holding a stock forever. Then you never have to pay taxes.

When you've got the mind-set to leave your investments alone, you don't stress over the day-to-day fluctuations. Many price moves come from events unrelated to a stock and have nothing to do with the well-being of the company. Rather, stocks in general can be hit because of a natural disaster or interest-rate hikes or a terrorist attack. If you own a major drug company, none of those events may have any relevance to your stock. But you can be sure the stock market, much like the tide with boats, will take all stocks down when these events happen. It's human nature to want to get away from anything risky when terrible things happen. You, on the other hand, will have the comfort of knowing what you own, be able to assess whether the news will affect your stocks, and make rational decisions. In fact, disasters will often bring opportunities for investors with the confidence to understand the transient nature of many news items. The key is to know which ones are short-lived and which ones can cause real damage.

The only way to know the difference is to know your stocks. Understand what markets they're in, who their customers are, whether interest rates will affect their cost of business or slow the demand for their products or services. In other words, really know your companies. Act like you're the CEO of each one. Get to know them as well as any officer of the firm. It takes some digging, but you have to do this part. If you aren't willing to do the work, you can't get to the Comfort Zone. Nobody gets a free pass.

The Web sites I've already given have plenty of information for you to understand a company. If you really want to get into the nuts and bolts of one, go to the SEC site (www.sec.gov) and read the annual and quarterly reports. Everything you want to know about the company is in these reports. Also use Value Line for some analysis of all the data. Check with your brokerage firm to see if it has research on the companies that you are interested in or already own. Keep up with the news on the stock by using the quote programs.

It sounds like a lot to do, but once you've got your investments made, you can focus on only your stocks or mutual funds. It only takes a few minutes a day to check the news headlines. And if you use the e-mail services of some of the news sites, the news will be in your e-mail in-box when you go online.

You can check once a day because you're not trying to trade the market. You don't need to have instant updates. Even though a stock price will move down after bad news, unless it's devastating, you don't want to sell the stock. If you determine that the news is only the beginning of more of the same, and do want to sell, you can do it the next day. This may cost you some money because if you had seen the news right away, you might have had a higher price when you sold. But this approach also works when the news is good. By not seeing it until later, the stock will most likely have moved up from the news, and if you decide to sell it, you will have made more money from the later information.

The point is, you're not trying to trade stocks, you're investing in them so you don't need total immersion in the market. Just like the gas station

I mentioned earlier in the book, you wouldn't expect its value to change a great deal from day-to-day. And real value is added over time—with more pumps or a restaurant or other additions that will bring incremental value. Stocks are like that too. The price you pay is for the company as it is now with some expectations for the future. You need to hang on to a stock for some time to see how the company grows and what new value goods or services added by the company provide to enhance your investment. That growth doesn't happen overnight. Don't expect your stock to move up dramatically unless there are reasons for it, such as breakthrough technology or a giant contract, or new gas pumps.

Be prepared to give your investments time to grow. You should spend a long time picking them. Hopefully, you'll choose the best stocks in their competitive sectors. Once you've made your decisions, and know why you made the decisions, let the companies go to work for you. Give them time to improve, to grow, to be even more profitable. Be a reluctant seller. When you own the best, until proven otherwise, you would only be trading down to a lesser stock if you sold.

Trading: For Those Who Must Learn on Their Own

Human nature being what it is, many readers, particularly ones new to investing, will have an urge—no, a need—to trade. They just know that the rules don't apply to them and that they are smarter than the average reader or even the average investor. They may very well be. But they still won't make money trading.

Having said that, some of you intrepid readers will want to trade anyway, if for no other reason than to prove me and the world wrong. With these readers in mind (I hope a small minority, because trading takes you away from your Comfort Zone), I will offer ten tips for trading that help you quickly move up the learning curve.

1. **Only trade liquid stocks, at least at first.** This means stocks that trade millions of shares a day. The more shares that trade, the more liquid they are, meaning you can get in and out easily. When you try trading smaller stocks, ones that trade less than 100,000 shares a

day, many times they will only trade 100 shares before the price moves up or down. If you have more than 100 shares to buy or sell, you will add to your costs of trading because the stock will move up or down based on your order, the last thing you want.

2. **Trade with the lowest commissions.** As mentioned earlier, commissions add up quickly when you trade. You need to keep this expense as low as possible if you're going to have a fighting chance. One online broker is down to $5 a trade on an unlimited number of shares if you qualify for its program (Brown & Co.). There are plenty at $7 to $10 a trade starting with Scottrade (www.scottrade .com) at $7. Be sure you can place "limit" orders for the same commission as "market orders." A limit order places a limit on the price at which you will buy or sell a stock. A market order is one that is executed at the market, regardless of that price. A "stop limit" order is one that is triggered when a certain price is attained, and you are only willing to buy or sell at that price.

3. **Don't trade anything but stocks.** If you even think about trading currencies or options or futures, put this book down and buy another. You don't want to be in a Comfort Zone. You want to be in the Totally Anxious Zone. The reason: All of these markets were developed for institutions. Small investors are only allowed in for their money. You don't have the mathematical skills or the offsetting positions that the institutions bring to these trades. You are truly in the wrong place at the wrong time whenever you venture into these trading pits.

4. **Trade stocks with small spreads.** The spread is the difference between the bid and the ask. The bid is what the market maker (on the NASDAQ) or the specialist (on the NYSE or AMEX) will pay for stock if someone wants to sell. The ask is the price those same traders will offer stock to anyone who wants to buy. In other words, when you want to sell, you get the bid, and when you buy, you pay the ask. The smaller the difference between the bid and the ask, the better your chance of making money because it doesn't take much

movement up to cover the spread and your commissions (always remember to add the commissions to your cost basis, the price you
paid for your stock). Many stocks are now traded with only a penny
or two spread between the bid and the ask. Some of the more famous ones are Lucent Technology, Nortel, Oracle, and Microsoft.
All of these are large, liquid stocks with relatively small spreads.

5. **Trade volatile stocks.** Not all stocks will move up or down with
enough enthusiasm to make money trading. Look at a stock's chart.
If it moves quickly, especially on the upside, this is what you're looking for. Also, check a stock's beta. The beta is a measure of the
volatility of a stock when its price movement is compared with the
Standard & Poor's 500 index over the last year. If a stock moves exactly the same as the index, the beta is 1. If it moves 20% more, up
and down, than the index, then the beta is 1.2. If it moves 20% less
than the index, the beta is .80. Stay away from the low beta stocks.
They're great for Comfort Zone investing, but terrible for trading.
The higher the beta, the better chance you have as a trader to see real
price movement. Most quote programs supply the beta on a stock.

6. **Don't short stocks.** Shorting stocks is best left to the professionals
or experienced traders. When you short a stock, you can literally
lose an infinite amount of money. There is no limit to your loss potential until you cover the trade. Also, you have to pay the dividend
of a stock that you're short. Shorting requires constant monitoring
and extreme due diligence to get it right.

To short a stock, you sell it without owning it. It must be borrowed by your broker to deliver to the party that bought the stock
you sold. When the price goes down, you can buy it back at a profit.
Then your broker can take the stock you bought and deliver it to the
broker from which it was borrowed. But if the stock goes up and up
and up, there is no end to the money you can lose. Don't try this
at home.

7. **Practice brutal discipline.** By this I mean you have to be willing to
take small losses a lot of the time. If there is one thing that separates

the true traders from the wannabes, it's the ability to admit an error and sell out of a stock. Most traders on Wall Street will not hold a position overnight. They want to be flat, or hold no stocks, when they leave the desk at night. That's because no one knows what will happen before stocks open again. Also, most traders have absolute levels of losses they will accept before getting out. That is, they determine that 5% is the most they're willing to lose and then they'll bail, no matter what the reason. That way, they will always have capital to trade. If they sell after a 5% loss and wait for a 10% gain before getting out, they will always, always make money. The reason this rule is so hard to follow is that emotions get in the way. Too often a trader will feel "this time it's different. If I just hang on, it will turn around, this one time." Most of the time it doesn't. If you want to trade, you need to establish your own "absolute rules." Determine the percentage you're willing to lose and stick with it, no matter how much you think it's different this time. It might be. But it could also be only the beginning of a slide that could wipe you out.

8. **Buy information.** If you want a fighting chance, you need real time information. That means buying a trading program such as Bridge (www.channel.bridge.com) or Bloomberg (www.bloomberg.com) or Reuters (www.reuters.com). They're expensive so you have to make enough money trading to cover these costs, but without a service with real-time quotes (the quotes you see on all the Web sites are delayed by at least 15 minutes, but your broker will have real-time quotes when you want to enter an order or check a price), you don't have any chance of making a profit trading. To put a twist on the old saying: When it comes to trading, what you don't know won't hurt you—it will kill you. You have to know what's going on, RIGHT NOW.

9. **Don't put all your money in one trade.** If you like an idea for a trade, buy 100 shares and see how it works. It raises the per share cost of your trades (if you're paying a flat $7 for an unlimited amount of shares, of course, buying more shares lowers your per share cost). But you're just learning this game. Think of it as a graduate school of

stocks. There's a tuition fee for learning, and there are no breaks for rookies. You're a rookie. It's a lot cheaper to learn on 100 shares than on 1,000.

10. **Start slow.** Take your time. Do plenty of "paper" trades, ones where you write down what you'd like to do, then just follow the action. See if you've got a feel for this. I recently read an article that said that psychopaths make the best traders because they take the emotion out of everything. It could be a good attribute to have in trading, but what a way to live! Bring the emotionless approach to trading and practice, practice, practice before you put real money to work. Remember, the most important key to winning at trading is discipline. If you don't keep your losses to a minimum on every trade, you won't play the game very long.

Now that you've got some tips on how to trade, let's hope you still won't do it. But if you do, you've got some of the odds more in your favor. Let's move on to tips on investing, a Comfort Zone activity.

Investing Tips

As I mentioned early in the book, I am sharing decades of experience with you, things I wish someone had told me when I started investing. I probably would have ignored them because I was cocky enough to think the rules didn't apply to me, that I was smarter than everyone who ever tried investing before I came along. The one thing investing teaches you is humility. I listen a lot better now. I hope you'll believe these tips apply to everyone. Yes, even you with the new MBA.

1. **Do your homework.** Seems obvious, but this is the core of good investing. It's very tempting to simply enter an order when a friend, especially a wealthy one, gives you a tip. But that tip may not be right for you. It might be highly speculative, somewhere Comfort Zone investors don't want to be. Investigate everything thoroughly. Know what you own extremely well. The better you know it, the more comfortable you're going to be owning it. And you'll know

whether certain news affects the business your stocks are in. Read as much as you can, not only about your stocks but about the economy in general. Get to know the jargon of investing. Maybe you'll find it interesting. If you don't, make sure you focus on only mutual funds because stocks demand understanding.

2. **Be a reluctant buyer and seller.** It's exciting to get into the world of investing. Most people want to buy a stock, to get their money working. Hang on to that enthusiasm and use it for due diligence. It's very easy to buy a stock. You just open an account at a brokerage firm or directly with a mutual fund and send in your money. But if you assume that your stock or mutual fund will go down if you don't know it well enough (it may or may not but pretend this is true because often enough it is), you won't be so quick to pull the trigger and buy something too soon. You can put this on a wall plaque and hang it in your office: I shall buy no stock before its time. The time is when you know it well enough to be comfortable. (Don't overthink this, however. Many investors get paralysis from analysis and never buy anything. There's a happy medium between ignorance and unending research. Find it.)

3. **Ease into your purchase.** Once you've done your research and have the best stock or mutual fund you can find, don't buy all of a position in one day. Buy one-third of the amount allocated, then watch the stock for a week and buy another third, then another week and the last third. Since you'll never buy at the bottom (or sell at the top), you have a chance to average your cost for the stock or fund. If the stock goes straight up from the first day you bought your initial position, congratulations, you win. You can add more at a higher price and hopefully watch it continue higher. But chances are very good that within a 3-week period, the stock will not go straight up. If it does, please call me.

4. **Invest in your investing.** You need information for better decisions but not the same information as a trader. You're looking for data, analysis of data, and most of all, ideas to research. Start with

a computer. If you don't have one, you're spending much more time than necessary to find good stocks. As mentioned earlier, the computer won't find you a winning stock with every pick, but it will let you screen out bad ones very quickly. The most basic information can come from free sites such as The Online Investor, MarketWatch, Yahoo!Finance, MSN Money, and many others, but to get plenty of news and help and databases, you need to pay. Subscribe to the online Wall Street Journal for $79 a year (www.wsj.com). This is one of the best bargains ever. Other good, basic resources are Value Line (www.valueline.com) for analysis and data and recommendations on stocks and/or Morningstar (www.morningstar.com) for mutual funds and stocks. Remember, knowledge is power, and it's also a comfort.

5. **Have patience, lots of patience.** As already mentioned, this is the rarest commodity on Wall Street. If you can discipline yourself to hang on to your great stocks through the rough times, you'll often see them rebound quickly and in large, upward moves. It seems just when I can't take the pain any longer, I sell a stock, and then it starts to recover. I don't know how the stock knows I've sold it, but it does. I'm sure you have similar stories. If you own great stocks, they will be the first to bounce back when the general market begins a recovery. Have the patience to hang on. And since you will never own too much of any one stock (remember to trim back positions that have too large of a percentage of your portfolio), the pain won't be so great if one or two stocks are getting trounced during a bad market. They won't throw you out of your Comfort Zone.

6. **There is more comfort in big than in small.** Even with the scandals at WorldCom, Enron, Tyco, and Adelphia, which were all large companies, the odds of your success are greater with larger companies because they have more capital to weather storms. While smaller companies can move quicker into new markets, they are always capital constrained and have no cushion to sit on during hard times. Capital matters. As B. C. Forbes once said, an idea without

capital is just an idea. When you have lots of capital, you can afford to try lots of ideas. Or, if times are bad, you don't have to try any because your basic business will continue to be profitable and add to capital. In assembling your Core Portfolio, strive to buy the best of the best and go for the very large stocks, with market caps of at least $5 billion. Most quote programs will give you the market cap in the box of data with a stock quote.

7. **Don't get emotionally involved.** Your stock doesn't love you so why should you love it? Emotions tend to take you out of a Comfort Zone, making you do things that rational minds wouldn't, like selling the first time the stock goes below where you bought. Or holding on to a stock that clearly has problems, such as major accounting irregularities, and will take years to recover. Stocks represent companies. Sometimes stocks trade in a world all their own, not reflecting anything to do with a company but reflecting the fear or euphoria that investors are feeling at the moment. If you accept the fact that the stock market does not always act rationally in the short run but will do so in the long run, you will see great opportunities while others only panic. In other words, if a large earthquake hits California and the stock market takes a dive for several days, it doesn't make sense that a stock that does business only east of the Mississippi goes down with the market. But it will. If that company is having a great year and you don't own too much of it already, this is a great opportunity to buy more.

8. **Don't let all the noise get to you.** Now that you understand better what the economic announcements mean, you can determine for yourself whether the latest unemployment numbers or a move in the Fed funds rate is meaningful or not. There will be plenty of experts telling you what they think and what you should do. Listen to all of them, but never make a buy or sell decision based on what others say. Think it through and determine for yourself if it's a good time to buy or sell. Just because everyone else is selling doesn't make it right. Furthermore, just because someone is screaming on television doesn't make what he or she says any truer.

One last thought: Some so called famous stock market predictors are only famous for being famous. In other words, they sound great on television but they have no track record for being more right than anyone else. Always listen with a detached sense of calm. Don't get caught up in other people's hype.

9. **I've said it before, and I'll say it again: Never, ever, ever be out of the stock market.** Don't try to time the market, thinking you can step out of it while it's going down, then cleverly step back in, at just the right time, to ride it back up. It doesn't allow for that. It can go down quite a bit for five and a half of the six and a half hours it trades in a day, and in the last hour, rally to close on the plus side. There are plenty of newsletters that will try to convince you that you can time the market but you can't. No one can. It's the same as telling the future because that's where the next trades take place. Stay in the market. It has a way of turning around and moving dramatically higher just when all hope seems lost. If you're out, you'll miss some of the easiest money. Your goal is to invest wisely, comfortably, not try to trade stocks or time the market. Stick with your goal. You can afford to stay in the market at all times because the money you've allocated to your investments is dedicated to long-term success. You shouldn't need this money for car payments or the mortgage or for paying off your credit cards on time every month. That money should come from your income or your savings, which should equal at least 6 months of living expenses. To be in the Comfort Zone, you do the basics. You take care of the essentials. You save, you allocate, you dedicate, you patiently wait. You never think you're smart enough to get in and out of the market and make a quick killing.

10. **You don't have to be extra smart to make money in the stock market.** Comfort Zone investing is much like blocking and tackling in football. It's very basic. It wins. When you follow these time-tested rules, you do well. You won't always buy a winning stock, but much of the time you will. Also, have confidence in your stock picking. It's a big part of winning in the market. You have to have the confidence

to buy when all others are selling if you're going to win big. Armed with the knowledge of this book and several others mentioned earlier (and in the resources section), you will develop the confidence to step in and buy when everyone else is dumping. You don't have to be a math genius to understand the basic numbers. Most of the math is done for you on the Web sites or Value Line or other services. You don't have to calculate any of them, but you do have to understand what the numbers mean.

12

Invest Like A Pro

Prior to that, I had been investing with
my glands instead of my head.

—*Warren Buffett*

Glands—or emotions—only cause trouble in the stock market. Getting too carried away, either by buying too quickly or too much, is the fast lane out of the Comfort Zone. Here are some tips the "ice cold" pros use to keep their hearts out and their heads in when they invest.

Always Look Ahead

The real pros aren't focused on what's happening today. That's already priced in the stock unless there's a huge surprise that no one figured in their calculations. The future is what counts to a real investor. Temporary problems, whether they're hurricanes or earthquakes or floods or terrorist attacks or fires or anything that temporarily shakes up a region or the psyche of investors, don't affect the real pros. They don't sell everything when those terrible events happen. They check their portfolios to see which individual companies they own are directly affected by the catastrophe, such as a property insurance company that sold a lot of policies in a hurricane-damaged area. That might be a good candidate for sale, unless the fact that the company will be raising rates to pay for the losses compensates for any temporary earnings interruption. If that's the case, then that stock will be a buy, not a sell, because the future will be more profitable.

It's the ability to look beyond what's happening today that greatly helps investors. Being able to keep your head while all others are losing theirs is a rare attribute. It's only human to join the herd, to buy when the market is moving up and sell when stocks are being dumped. But looking ahead allows you to see what others don't. Focusing on exactly how a problem of today will affect the company tomorrow will often times allow you to be a buyer when many others are selling. Don't get too caught up in today. Focus on the potential of each company well beyond the current events.

Dare to Tread Where Others Fear

There's a group of investors known as contrarians. They like to buy when everyone else is selling. Contrarians, of course, can be wrong. The reason everyone is selling may be lost on them, and a stock being dumped may never come back. But many times, stocks currently out of favor come back with a vengeance. If you have the nerve to step in, after doing your due diligence, you are often highly rewarded.

That's because stocks will move on emotions. Two of them. One is fear, and the other is greed. When fear grips the market, valuations on stocks become so attractive that smart investors wonder what is going on. They can't believe people would be willing to sell a great stock for such a low price. But sellers aren't thinking. They're simply reacting, selling a stock that is low because they've seen it wither and erode their net worth. They can't take it anymore. They sell it. Those investors will not make a lot of money.

True investors see adverse times as great opportunities. They actually like it when stocks are pounded to levels that make no sense. They become like kids in a candy shop, not knowing which ones to grab first. There are bargains everywhere. They have the ability to move in opposition to the tide, daring to believe in themselves and their due diligence. It takes true grit to do that, but large sums of money are made that way.

If you are fully invested when the stock market has a meltdown, you can use it as a time to weed out your underperforming stocks. Sell them and buy the great ones you've always wanted at bargain prices. You most likely will take a loss on your sale, but you're upgrading your portfolio to better stocks. You'll make a lot more when they lead the market on the way up. Dare to be a buyer when everyone else is a seller—but only if you've done your homework.

Price Is Your Best Friend

The pros don't just put in an order to buy a stock or to sell one. They know exactly the price they want to pay or the price they want to sell. They let the stock come to them. They don't chase after it if it rallies. They don't panic and hit the bids (sell) if it's faltering. They have price levels for when they want to buy and to sell.

You should, too. After you've done your homework on a stock, determine what you want to pay for it. In fact, make a list of 20 stocks you'd like to buy and the price you're willing to pay. That way you won't be focused on just one, anxiously waiting for it to get to your price.

You can keep track of potential buys in portfolio tracker programs available on AOL, MarketWatch, Yahoo!Finance, MSNMoney, or other financial Web sites. You can even set alarms. When a stock reaches a certain level, you'll get an e-mail alert.

To establish your prices, use a method that makes sense to you. You want to be as calculating as you can on this one. Take as much of the guesswork out as you can. Use standard valuations such as Price to Book or Price to Earnings or other ratios that are fully explained in the books I recommended earlier. Again, you have to do that homework if you're going to invest successfully. I wish there were a shortcut, but you have to know the rules of the game if you're going to play.

Buying stocks with limits is a lot like fly fishing. Many times you don't get anything. At other times you can't believe your good fortune. If you have a long list of great stocks with prices that you've established as buys, when you do catch one, you'll be extremely happy.

Due Diligence

I've mentioned due diligence often. That's because it's so damned important. The pros know more about companies, their competition, and their potential than many CEOs. Of course, the pros do this for a living. They spend their days finding out everything they can before investing. You, on the other hand, have a day job. You don't have the same access to management. You don't have the same level of research.

However, you do have enough information resources to make good decisions. If you use analytical services like Value Line in conjunction with data from Web sites, you can pick winning stocks. Don't think you have to know everything before buying a stock. You can't. That's an impossible goal.

You do need to know revenue growth, earnings, markets served, competition—all the basics that are provided on the Web sites or in newsletters. There are some things you will never know. For example, one of the critical elements to a bank's well-being is the quality of the loans it makes. One measure of that is the Loan to Value Ratio. That ratio is not provided in any database. The only way you get a real look at the quality of loans is by seeing the bank's loan portfolio, to see the losses they take from bad loans. The only problem with that is those numbers are released quarterly so you can be months behind in what's going on in the bank. But the pros don't see those numbers either so you're not at a competitive disadvantage.

The point is that you can do very good, efficient due diligence. You can get to at least 80% of what the pros see. You won't see the detail or the analysis they get from institutional research, but you can still make great investments with information available to the general public.

Don't Fight the Fed

This is an old Wall Street saying. It means that when the Fed is tightening interest rates, it's better to be defensive in your stock positions. You want to own consumer staples, drugs—the industries that aren't as sensitive to interest-rate changes. When the Fed is loosening interest rates, it's time to be aggressive, to own banks, home builders, construction equipment manufacturers, the industries that benefit from lower rates.

That's why you'll want to follow what the Fed is doing. Not that you have to read the minutes from each FOMC (Federal Open Market Committee) meeting. Just check the business pages or watch CNBC to listen to commentators on which way rates are going. You'll want to adjust your portfolio accordingly so you won't fight the Fed. The Fed will move the markets, and you want to be on the same side as the biggest mover and shaker on earth. Remember, when the Fed changes the direction of interest rates, that begins a cycle that usually last several years.

Spread Risks

I've already described a Core Portfolio. The whole idea behind it is to spread your risk so that no matter what interest rates do or what disasters hit, your wealth won't be overly affected. That doesn't mean you won't see your stocks go down when the market is in the tank. But with good risk dispersion, you should outperform the stock market—always a worthy goal.

The pros know the most important element of investing is to have enough capital to continue to invest. By spreading their risk throughout many sectors, they know they will never get wiped out because oftentimes what is bad for one sector is good for another. Keep your risk to a minimum with enough diversity in stocks and mutual funds to stay in your Comfort Zone and preserve your capital.

Buy Companies with Revenues

This sounds self-evident, but it isn't. In particular there are segments of the market that don't have revenues for many, many years. Some of the companies in those segments don't ever sell anything. They go bankrupt.

That's why you want to always buy stocks with revenues. It will keep you out of a lot of problems. You want to focus on the companies with increasing revenues.

The reason I want to spend a little time on this is because the biotech industry will be calling you, loudly. You will hear of the next breakthrough in cancer treatment or a cure for the common cold. It will be something that sounds so good you'll break your wrist trying to grab your money to throw money at the company. Do not, I repeat, do not buy these stocks.

But you probably will anyway. So have the discipline to only buy the ones with the highest revenues. In the biotech world, that would be Genentech or Amgen, as of this writing. Or if you absolutely cannot resist the story behind a stock, buy less than 1% of your total portfolio of it. If you have that as your maximum exposure, you can still stay in your Comfort Zone. Trust me, after going through decades of owning a few biotech stocks that are always just that close to an amazing new discovery, I only buy small amounts of great stories and large amounts of great revenues.

Always Stay in the Game

The pros know you have to play the game to win it. You can't be watching on the sideline, hoping you can time your entry at the bottom of a cycle. You can't do that. No one can. Real investors know the pain of watching a great stock go down and down and down without good reason. They don't sell. They buy more if they can. They don't dump the stock or jump out of the market just because everybody else is.

This is one of the hardest rules to follow because the agony of feeling your stock drop every day is much like salt being sprinkled in an open wound, followed by vinegar, every five minutes, while your head is surrounded with mosquitoes, and the sun is baking your feet. In other words, it hurts. And one sure way to relieve the pain is to sell out of your stocks, get out altogether, and let the market go where it wants.

It's about the time you decide to sell that the market has an uncanny way of turning around and heading up. Instead of selling everything, the best way to lessen the pain is to lighten your positions, make strategic, defensive moves, or have less money in the market. All of these moves are fine. Just don't give up and get out of everything. You'll find it hard to get back in because your mind will be haunted with images of stock prices going lower and lower and lower. When you do decide to make your move back in, you'll have a tendency to wait until a stock gets a little lower, wait until the price has stopped going down.

The stock may not go lower. And trying to time the bottom for a stock's price is impossible. But if you've done your homework and have a price in mind that makes the stock a bargain, you can buy with confidence. You hope you're buying at the bottom. It doesn't matter. You've made a judgment that if you can buy the stock at your price, you're happy. You're comfortable. You're back in your Comfort Zone.

13

Four Ways to Invest and a Few Words About IRAs

I have made good judgments in the past. I have made good
judgments in the future.

—*J. Danforth Quayle, former vice president of the United States*

You'll need to make good judgments to find and stay in your Comfort Zone. One of them is how to invest. By that I mean, how do you actually buy or sell a stock or a mutual fund? What are the costs? What are the advantages of one way over another?

Investing Basics

Now that you've read how to pick good stocks, mutual funds, and bonds, you have to actually execute your strategy. You need to buy some or all of your picks. In order to buy stocks, you need to have an account with a stock brokerage firm (unless you are buying a stock directly from a company). Your brokerage firm will take your order and place it on the correct exchange or send it to a market maker in the stock you want to buy.

The exception: You can buy a number of stocks directly from companies.

Most of them are the larger ones. You contact the XYZ Corp. and ask for the Investor Relations Department. They explain how to send in your money. There are no commissions when you buy directly from a company, but then selling your stock back to the company can be complicated, if allowed at all. I don't recommend buying stocks directly because it limits your buying and selling in many different ways, all of which are bad for you. The only good thing about this approach is saving commissions. But commissions at online brokers are so low that the advantage isn't worth much.

The vast majority, more than 99.9% of stocks, are bought through brokers. You can buy and sell within seconds. You pay a commission but receive great liquidity and very fast execution of your orders as well as excellent record keeping of your transactions. You'll need to pick a broker, either a full-service or a discount/online broker. I'll explain both later in this chapter.

Mutual funds, on the other hand, can be bought and sold relatively easily, directly from the mutual fund. You simply call them up, establish an account by sending in your money, then you can buy the fund whenever you wish. When you want to sell, you also call, tell them to sell, and you can have your money back within a few days. You can also buy and sell mutual funds through brokers which, again, I recommend because of the ease of the transaction and the tracking of your holdings. Many mutual funds can be bought at a broker with no fees. Each broker has a list of the funds they represent without charging commissions.

A few other basics to know: When you buy a stock on the New York Stock Exchange, your order goes to the central trading floor of the NYSE and a specialist in the stock buys or sells your stock, acting on the order from your broker. There is a specialist for every stock on the NYSE. It's their job to maintain an orderly market in a stock. For a full history and more information on the exchange, please go to its Web site www.nyse.com. All NYSE and American Stock Exchange (AMEX) stocks have one, two, or three letters in their symbols. Very few stocks trade on the AMEX.

If you buy a stock traded through NASDAQ (National Association of Securities Dealers Automated Quote System), your order goes to a market maker who is bidding the highest for your stock when you enter your order to sell or offering it at the lowest price when you want to buy a stock.

The main distinction between the NYSE and the NASDAQ is that there is no central exchange floor for NASDAQ. It is made up of individual dealers who make a market in a stock, called market makers. Not all market makers trade in all NASDAQ stocks. In fact, none does. All NASDAQ stocks have four or five letters in their symbols. Stocks traded on the NASDAQ program are often more volatile and have wider spreads (the difference between the bid and the ask on a stock) than stocks traded on the NYSE. This shouldn't deter you from buying NASDAQ stocks, but be aware that sometimes you'll have more volatility with NASDAQ stocks because some of them trade with only a few market makers.

You should also know quote programs on Web sites give you bids and offers that are between 15 and 20 minutes old. If you go in to buy or sell a stock, it will most likely have a different price from what you see on your computer. For that reason, you need to always ask your broker for the current market price when you enter an order. Then you won't be surprised when the price you see on your confirmation is higher or lower than what you see on your screen.

You can also use an online broker who will give you a real-time quote on a stock when you enter an order. Then you know where your stock is trading as you enter the order. If you use a full-service broker, he or she can also give you a real-time quote when you enter your order.

Another small thing: When you buy a stock, your money doesn't go to the company. Your stock is being sold by someone who wants out of the very same stock you want to buy. Think about that sometime. You might wonder what he or she knows that you don't.

A Full-Service Broker

A very good way to learn about the stock market is to use a full-service broker. I recommend using one if you know nothing about the stock market or investing. You can learn a lot from a full-service broker. Of course, you're going to pay for the knowledge in the form of higher commissions and more fees. But if you absolutely do not want to use a computer and invest by yourself, then use a stockbroker. And get your money's worth.

Understand up front that the only reason you use a broker is to get stock recommendations and help with your investing. Also know that finding a good broker is about as hard as finding a good, honest auto mechanic. So the first thing you need to do is ask your friends and family what brokers they use and if they're happy with them—not because the broker is nice and takes them to lunch but because he or she makes money for clients. Good brokers always put their clients ahead of their own commissions, buying the right security to meet the client's needs, not the stock with the best payout to the broker. These brokers are hard to find, but they are out there. When you can find one that works for you, grab him or her and get to work.

By the way, it doesn't matter where that broker lives. Your investments are safe anywhere in the country. You're much better served by using a good broker who lives thousands of miles away if he or she makes you money and communicates well. You don't need to see them weekly or monthly or even quarterly. Once a year would probably be plenty as long as you're talking or e-mailing or writing regularly about your needs, and you're getting information and recommendations as you want them.

I'm thinking in particular of a stockbroker in Oregon to whom I would not hesitate giving my money if I needed a broker. Since I've been an investment advisor, I feel I can manage my own money and use an online broker comfortably. But if I needed a broker, I would contact him, even though I live in California, and talk to him about helping me invest. The most important element of the relationship has already been established: I trust him, have watched what he does with other clients, and know he puts their needs first.

You will be well advised to spend a great deal of time interviewing stockbrokers and finding one that you enjoy and feel a sense of trust in. Of course, if you can avoid it, don't talk to any that haven't been recommended. It will save you a lot of time. If, however, you decide you want a local brokerage firm to help you, then this is the process you'll go through: You'll call the firm and ask to speak to a stockbroker because you want to open a new account. You'll be transferred to the stockbroker on duty. This is a man or woman who is usually new to the firm and is looking to build a book—a client list large enough to make a living. This person may be fabulous; but most of the time, you should know, the best stockbrokers only work with referrals from their clients. They do not take cold calls. They don't have "day duty." So the odds are against you going in for finding a good broker this way.

Let's assume you make an appointment with the broker of the day and head in for an interview. You should definitely meet this person because you're about to enter into a very close, very personal relationship. You want to see if you feel comfortable with the broker, to see if he or she listens well. You can't know about the trust issue in one interview. That happens over time. But you'll have a visceral reaction to whomever you meet. Go with your gut. If you don't get the right feeling, thank him or her for the time. Then the next day, call and ask for the manager, explain that you'd like to meet another broker. Go through the same process again.

As to which firms are best, that's a hard one because a great broker is your key to success, not the firm where he or she works. While the biggest houses, like Merrill Lynch, Morgan Stanley, and SmithBarney have great resources, they often require a very high minimum amount to open an account, sometimes as much as $2 million. If you're not in that bracket, you might still be able to open an account, but you won't get a personal stockbroker, something you definitely need if you're new to investing.

That's why some of the regional firms like AG Edwards, Edward Jones, and Piper Jaffray deserve your attention. They specifically cater to smaller investors. While they don't have research staffs as large as the bigger firms, they do have ample resources to supply you with ideas and execute your orders.

Here's the deal with stockbrokers: They're paid on commissions. That is, they have to write tickets to buy or sell securities to make money. Some firms pay a small percentage to their brokers for bringing in assets, but that's not where the money is made for a broker. Without buying and selling stocks, they don't keep their jobs very long. So the system works against the broker who doesn't want to trade your account. That's why so many good brokers leave the business and become advisors (see below for more on them). That way there is no conflict of interest.

Knowing how your broker is paid will help you understand how they think and why they recommend stocks to you. That means you always have to be very clear about your objectives and what you want. Sometimes you have to repeat your goals to your broker because they're sometimes forgotten.

Using a full-service stockbroker is a great way to begin the investing process. You can learn much from research reports as well as listening to your broker explain why things are appropriate for your portfolio. The one thing you should never do is take a recommendation from your broker and then buy or sell that stock through an online broker. That isn't fair. Your stockbroker is working for you, the firm is providing resources for you, and the deal is that you pay them for it.

And you will pay. A trade that would cost you $7 at an online broker may end up costing you $250 or more at a full-service broker if there are thousands of shares in the trade. That's what I mean by paying for the full service. But if you hold that stock for a long time and it's a winner, your broker has earned the commission.

One final comment about full-service brokers: Beware of their own mutual funds. There are a few reasons for that. First, these mutual funds will often buy stocks when the firm has positioned a large block of a particular stock and then can't sell it. It gets stuck into these mutual funds. This can be particularly true if the firm has a new issue, an initial public offering (IPO), that isn't moving. A convenient way to make sure it sells well is to put it into the in-house mutual fund. That's not always in your best interest.

The second is that these mutual funds will always have high transaction fees when you buy and/or sell them. In other words, where other mutual funds have no transaction fees or initial "loads" (a load is the upfront fee to buy a fund), these funds can charge between 5% and 10% of your investment just to get into them.

The third point, and the one that really is the worst: These funds are not transferable, and they don't trade anywhere else. That means if you decide to leave the brokerage firm, you can't take that fund with you. You have to sell it, and there is a large transaction fee attached to that. So if you're leaving the firm because you're unhappy with the performance, the service, for whatever reason, this will be the salt in the wound because you have no choice. You must sell the fund, and it has to be done with the broker you're leaving.

Let me make a blanket statement: Never let your broker sell you an in-house mutual fund, one that has the firm's name on it. There are plenty of others that will give you as good or better performance that allow you to buy and sell them without large fees, and they are transferable to other firms.

One more important issue: DO NOT, DO NOT, DO NOT give your broker "discretion" over your account. Discretion means your broker can buy and sell whatever he wants, whenever he wants, thereby producing lots of commissions for him, rarely any profits for you. You need to sign a power of attorney for your broker to have discretion. Be sure you don't sign anything like that. In fact, the best brokers never ask for discretion over accounts because it often leads to lawsuits.

Your account is totally within your control. Do not give up that control to anyone. Always make sure your broker carefully explains any recommendation, and that you give specific permission for any transaction, buy or sell, within your account. You'll avoid a lot of losses and maybe lawsuits that way. If you feel you want to give up control of your money, then buy a mutual fund or use an investment advisor (more on those in this chapter). Stockbrokers are not investment advisors nor are they money managers, even though some are called financial advisors or financial consultants. They are paid to sell stocks, mutual funds, annuities, and other products. They get paid on commissions. Please remember that when working with them.

I don't want to leave full-service brokers on a negative note. They serve people well, sometimes, but only if people ask a lot of questions and make brokers earn their money. If your personality is such that you want to have someone help you, need someone to hold your hand through the learning process of investing, then by all means use a full-service broker, preferably one who has been recommended by a friend or family member who is very happy with his or her broker's performance, not just their personalities.

One last thought. When you decide to open an account, choose the Margin Account option, unless you don't trust yourself with the temptation. If you decide to borrow money in your Margin Account (and only for a short period of time), you have the paper work done. You will find greater flexibility with this account, which has all the features of a cash account if you want to use it like a cash account but with the added benefit of quicker access to your money. Again, just because you have a Margin Account doesn't mean you have to use it. But if you need or want to use the margin benefits, they're easily accessed if the account is already open.

Online Brokers

I admit it up front: I really like these brokers. They fit my personality and my pocketbook. They charge considerably less for buying and selling stocks or mutual funds. They have great information. I control the entire process. I never have to talk to a broker or hear a sales pitch. If you're able to research ideas on your own and feel comfortable in making decisions independently, you'll feel right at home with an online broker.

The online brokers are consolidating as this is being written. There are now about five major brokers online: Scottrade, Charles Schwab, E*Trade, Ameritrade, and Fidelity. There are many other names like Brown & Co., Harris Direct, Web Street, and TradeScape (all owned by E*Trade), or TD Waterhouse, Datek Online, JB Oxford, National Discount Brokers, and Bidwell (all owned by Ameritrade), but they are no longer independent. How this will affect commission rates and services has yet to be seen, but if there are only three or four left, there may be higher commissions from on-line brokers as they have the power to lift rates without heavy competition. On the other hand, if they raise rates too high, then new firms will start up and offer the same services at lower commissions.

Commissions at online brokers can run as low as $5 a trade, regardless of the shares, up to $29.95 a trade for 100 shares of stock and even much higher at some firms when thousands of shares are involved. However, if you are an active investor or have a large account, those rates come down fast. But sometimes you have to ask for lower rates, so don't hesitate to do so.

Most online brokers use their name for their Web site pages. For example, Scottrade is found at www.scottrade.com. If you go to their site, you find out quickly their main features: $7 per trade, no account fees, $500 minimum to open an account, no limit as to the number of shares you can trade for $7. They have hundreds of branches around the country to help you open an account or answer your questions if you want to talk with someone face to face.

You can open your account online with any of the brokers. You click on the Open Your Account Now button, and you'll go to a page full of questions. The account you want, as with a full-service broker, is the Margin Account. That allows you more flexibility with your money in case you need or want it. You have to send in an initial deposit (a check is best, never cash) by registered mail or deliver it to a local branch before you can buy stocks or mutual funds. That deposit is immediately credited to your account so you can buy stock on the same day you make the deposit. You can not, however, get a check from the account until the deposit check clears.

Most of the online brokers, and particularly Scottrade, have separate pages that explain each type of account, such as the differences between a Roth IRA and a traditional IRA. They explain what a SEP is (Simplified Employee Pension plan) as well as a Rollover IRA and a Coverdell ESA. If you have any questions, you can e-mail them directly or call a broker. Opening an account is extremely easy.

Once you've funded the account, you'll be able to buy or sell stocks or mutual funds online. You simply go to the Web site, enter your account ID and a password. That opens the account. If you want to buy a stock, it's this simple: Go the Trading page, just labeled Trade in some firms. It will ask for the following information:

The symbol of the stock

(The symbol is found by using the Symbol Lookup box provided by most quote programs or the broker's quote service.)

The number of shares

Enter the number you wish to buy or sell.

Action

The choices are Buy, Sell, Sell Short. Since you won't be selling short right away, if ever and not before you've had years of experience in the market, that leaves only the two most basic actions: buy or sell.

Order Type

Here are the types of orders:

- **Market.** This is where you want the broker to sell your stock at whatever the market will pay for it (the bid side of the market) or buy a stock at the market (the offer or ask side of the market). When you enter this type of order, you will see the real-time quote for the stock so you'll know almost exactly what you'll be getting. But you don't know exactly because stocks can move very fast and by the time you get your order in, the bid or offer side of the market may have moved. Until you get a confirmation back (by checking the Order Status of the trade that is part of the trading pages), you won't know what your final price is, either for a buy or a sell. Use a Market order on most stocks except ones that don't trade very much. Then you'll want to use a limit order.

- **Limit.** An order that limits the buy or sell of a stock to the price you stipulate. When you check Limit order, you need to enter the price you want to pay or, if you're selling, the price you want for your stock. Sometimes, when you use a limit order, the stock will trade at your price but you won't get a confirmation of the trade. That's because your stock didn't trade, someone else's did. There are two reasons for that. First, someone may have stipulated the same price as you did and was there before you were. Trading is done on a first come, first served basis. Or, and this is especially true when your stock trades on the NASDAQ, the stock was never bid at your price if you're a seller, or no one offered the stock at your price if you're a buyer. In other words, the trades that happened at your price were not on your side of the market. That means someone sold stock at your price, which was the bid side of the market. The market maker bid that price. But you were a buyer at that price and no market maker offered the stock at your price, only bid at your price. There are rules now that allow you to be the best bid but only if your broker makes a market in the stock you are buying. In other words, you can be ahead of your broker. The broker can't buy stock before it fills your order in stocks it makes a market in. This sounds a little confusing, but it is very straightforward if you think about it for a while since you buy on the offer side of the market and sell on the bid side. If no market maker offers you stock at your price or bids for stock at your price, you don't get a trade done. If you understand this, you won't feel so frustrated with the NASDAQ system and the way Limit orders work.

- **Stop order.** This is a price you enter that triggers a buy or a sell. These are usually used to limit losses. You enter a Stop order above the market for a buy and below the market for a sale. The buy Stop usually has to do with short selling so let's not take time on that. The sell Stop order is a way of stopping your losses. In other words, if you're worried a stock might be hurt by a pending news announcement (a contract award or quarterly update), you can use a Stop order to protect your profits or limit your losses. Say the stock is trading at $10 a share before the news you're expecting. You don't know how the stock will trade afterward, but you don't want to lose a profit if it goes down dramatically. You can enter a Stop order at $9.75 or some other number close to but below $10. That way, if the news is bad and the stock trades off, your order will be triggered if the stock sells at $9.75. When it trades there, your order is automatically entered as a sell order. IT DOESN'T MEAN YOU WILL GET $9.75 FOR YOUR STOCK. It means you will hit the next bid for the stock and be out of it. The next bid may be $9.50 if the stock is really tanking, or it may be $9.80 if it's bouncing off $9.75. Whatever the next bid is for the stock, that's what you'll get for your stock. If you have an order in for more than 100 shares, and the stock is thinly traded, you will most likely get several different prices for each lot of 100 shares, but you will get out of the stock. The Stop order can give you a great deal of comfort if you're going on vacation or are unable to watch your stock when news is announced. If you have a Stop order protecting your profits, you can watch a stock go higher with no concerns. Or if it has a problem and starts to tumble, you can relax. With a Stop order, you'll be out of it, and into your Comfort Zone.

- **Stop Limit order.** The Stop Limit order is just like the Stop order except that it limits the price action. In other words, you are telling your broker you want to sell when the stock gets to a certain price (the "Stop" part of the order), but then you only want to sell at a limit, or a specified price (the "Limit" part of the order). These sound great in theory; and if executed, they're wonderful. But here's the catch: Many Stop orders are triggered and then the next bid is below where you put in your Limit. For example, using the same $10 stock from above, if you put in your Stop Limit order at $9.75, here's what might happen. The stock will trade at $9.75 so your Stop will be in effect. But then it may be bid at $9.70 or $9.65 while your Limit is $9.75. So you won't have a trade. If the stock continues to trade down, even though you had a Stop Limit order in place, you will not have sold your stock because the bid was never $9.75 and that was your limit on where you would sell. Take some time to understand this because a Stop Limit can give you a false sense of comfort if you don't. It's great to get your price when you want to sell, but using a Stop Limit order doesn't always make that happen. If you really want to be protected from a large downside move in a stock's price, only use the Stop order, not the Stop Limit order. The Stop Limit gives you false comfort while the Stop order is the real thing.

There are a few more boxes to fill on the Trading page, including:

Timing

There are four choices: Day Only; Good Til Canceled (GTC); Fill or Kill; Immediate or Cancel.

- **The Day Only command is exactly that.** It keeps your order in for the day you request to buy or sell a stock. For example, if a stock is trading at $10 a share and you want to buy it at $9.50, you will put in the price of $9.50 (you don't need to put in a Limit order because your buy is below the market; if it were above, you would need to put in a buy Stop order). You would also click on the Day only option. This is actually the default selection for orders. If you don't specify anything, you will automatically have a Day order. That's all you want to use 99% of the time.

- **GTC, or Good Til Canceled.** This order stays in effect for at least 90 days or until you cancel it. It may get you into trouble. Here's how: Let's take that trade above, where you want to buy a stock at $9.50. If that stock announces something horrible after the close of trading, and you have an open order to buy the stock at $9.50, the stock may be halted without trading the next day until a price level can be established where trades will occur. No matter what level that is, you will buy the stock the next day at your price of $9.50, even though the stock might open at $8 a share or lower. You can't cancel a GTC order once a stock has been halted for trading. You're stuck.

  The only time it might be acceptable to use a GTC order is if you're going on vacation, and you don't want to miss a certain price level. Then you could enter your order to buy or sell at whatever price you want. If it trades at your price, then you've either bought or sold it. But you run the risk of having some terrible news or some great news happen. For example, say you enter your Sell order at $12 on that $10 stock above. If the company announces it is being bought out at $20, you will sell your stock at $12 and miss out on a nice profit. I don't recommend ever using the GTC order. The cost can be too high.

- **The Fill or Kill order.** This order tells the trader of your stock that you want your order filled in its entirety or you want to kill the order. This is a factor when someone wants to buy or sell a large quantity of stock and doesn't want the order broken up. Say the order is to buy 10,000 shares of ZYX. If you specify the order as Fill or Kill, then the specialist in ZYX has to sell you 10,000 shares or nothing at all. He can't sell you 5,000 shares at your price and hope to sell you more later. Your order specifies that you wanted it all filled at your price or you're going to Kill the order.

- **The Immediate or Cancel order.** This order tells the same trader that he has to do it right now or the order is canceled. In other words, you don't want to wait around. You need your order filled this moment. You don't want to worry about the market fluctuating and losing this opportunity. And if you don't get your order filled right now, you're not going to let it sit there and have it support the stock (if it's a buy order) or weigh on the stock (if it's a sell order). You want in or out now, not a few seconds from now. Individuals rarely use this order, but it's there if you feel it will help you.

I have never used it because if I'm buying a stock with a Limit order, I want to fill the order and own the stock. How long it takes doesn't bother me. The same is true when I go to sell with a Limit order. I will wait for the buyers to come in at my price, even if it takes longer than I would like. My objective is to buy or sell the stock, and sometimes that takes time.

More Options

There are a couple more choices to make before you enter your order.

- **Dividend Reinvestment.** This instructs the broker to reinvest the dividend by buying the same stock that issued the dividend with the payment received from the stock. Or not. In which case, you receive the cash. Dividend reinvestment can be a great way to go if you don't need the cash and love a stock that you hold for a long time. That way you will buy the stock with your dividend (and no commissions) when it is sometimes very low and therefore more shares at a lower price, or fewer shares at a higher price. The bad part of the program is that it buys small amounts. Some even have partial shares. These can be rather messy in the portfolio.

  REMEMBER THIS: You have to keep track of each purchase price for tax purposes. When you sell a stock, each dividend reinvestment purchase has a separate price. Your gains and losses will be different for each one. It can be tough to find the cost basis for each stock bought unless you keep very good records. Your broker will have those buys on record, and online brokers keep a history of your account up to two years, which you can access. But if you own the stock for more than two years, you will most likely pay a special fee to get that information. If you use the Dividend Reinvestment feature, be sure to keep your own records. I don't use this feature because it makes tax time harder than it needs to be.

- **Special Conditions.** If you're entering nonmarket orders (ones that have conditions on them like the Limit orders), then you have choices as to how you want those orders executed.

- **Minimum Quantity.** This is the minimum number of shares you will accept. Say you want to buy 500 shares of ZYX, but you don't want some odd lots, like 14 shares. With this order option, you can specify that you will only take 100 shares at a time or 200 or whatever number you specify. This is helpful if you have a Limit order in and only fill part of the order. You won't have any odd lots dumped on you (odd lots are any trades with less than 100 shares). Odd lots used to be a problem because they would get lower bids and require higher offers to get executed. These days, odd lots are traded the same as round lots (100 shares minimum with 100 share increments). Your commission is always figured at the end of the day, on the total number of shares bought. You are not charged for each trade.

  Of course, the risk you take is that you won't get your order filled if you don't take everything that is offered, no matter what the size of the order. I've had plenty of orders take much of the day and taken in lots of 14 or 289 or whatever but when it's all over, I've bought the stock. I don't use the Minimum Quantity option because it doesn't bother me to have odd lots.

- **Do Not Reduce.** Also known as the DNR order, this order is for GTC orders where the stock has a dividend payment. If you instruct your broker to use the DNR, it means you don't want the price at which you enter to buy or sell a stock to be reduced by the amount of the dividend that is paid. Since a stock's price is reduced by the amount of the dividend paid at the opening of the trading day on the ex-dividend date, the order you have placed to buy that stock would naturally be affected by that dividend unless you specify

DNR. Here's an example: You have an order to sell ZYX at $10.25 a share. It closes on Monday at $10 a share and on Tuesday, it is ex-dividend for 25 cents. (Ex-dividend means, literally, without the dividend. In other words, if you own the stock on Monday, you will get the dividend. If you buy it on Tuesday, you'll have to wait another quarter to get it because the stock is trading ex-dividend, without the dividend.) That means the stock will open on Tuesday at $9.75 ($10 less the 25 cent dividend). Since you have designated your order to be DNR, you will not have your price reduced by the dividend amount of 25 cents. You want to have the dividend and get your $10.25 per share. If you don't designate the DNR, your Limit order will automatically be reduced by the amount of the dividend. In this case, that would be to $10 a share.

And That's About It

That's all you need to know to enter an order online. It seems like a lot to understand, and for the new investor, it will take a while. But study these pages, and you'll get it. Knowing these details will put you a long way into your Comfort Zone when it comes to buying and selling stocks or mutual funds.

Investment Advisors

Investment advisors used to be only for multimillionaires who could spare a million or two to give to a professional to invest in the stock market. Times have changed. Now you can have the same quality of management for much smaller amounts.

For example, Schwab has a program that will introduce you to an advisor near you if you have at least $100,000 to invest. Those advisors have registered with Schwab as wanting new clients and are willing to take that amount as a minimum.

Or you can ask your friends if they use an advisor and what the minimum is for their advisors. Sometimes, if you're referred by a client, the advisor will lower the minimum amount.

You'll want to consider an advisor if you have more than $100,000 to invest and don't want any of the responsibility of managing it. The advisor will make all the decisions to buy and sell stocks, bonds, and mutual funds. Some advisors only buy mutual funds. Be aware that you are paying an advisor fee and then the fund is taking a fee for its management. So you're paying double fees for the management of your money. If the advisor's performance has been outstanding, then those fees are worth it.

Other advisors specialize in one type of investing or sector of the market. For example, I know an advisor who only works in bank stocks. These are fine if you allocate a portion of your money to that type of advisor but not all of it since you won't get diversification from a specialist.

The most important part of finding a good advisor is references. If you go to Schwab or your friends or even the phone book, you'll find names of advisors. Talk to several of them. Get comfortable with them. The process is the same as for finding a stockbroker. But before you give them a single dollar, get at least three references and find out a few things: Investigate the performance of the advisor over several years, not just the last one. Sometimes an advisor's style doesn't work in very good markets but is a happy surprise in bad ones. Or vice versa. Find out if the advisor is punctual in communicating the quarterly report. Find out the fees, all of them, that will be charged. Most important, find out if clients are satisfied with their overall experience with the advisor.

Some advisors are great with communicating but terrible with performance. Or they'll present great returns but never seem to get around to sending you an update on your holdings. You're seeking an advisor that has it all, but if you have to compromise on something, make it in the communications department. Great performance is extremely hard to find; and if you can get outstanding returns on your investments, then make that your priority.

Again, you want to use an advisor if you don't want the day-to-day responsibility of managing your investment money. Advisors earn their fees. They do research, keep records, comply with NASD regulations, and keep you informed on a regular basis. Expect to pay about 1% to 1.5% of assets under management, depending on the size of your portfolio.

Advisors are a great way to go if they're the right ones. There are no tests they need to take, but registered advisors need to file with the SEC and the NASD and are subject to regular inspections. You will be given a copy of their NASD filing if you are seriously considering one. In it, you'll find out the background of the advisor. I recommend reading it carefully. But of course, you wouldn't seriously consider the advisor unless he or she has already been highly recommended or had fabulous references.

Advisors are a great way to get to your Comfort Zone quickly if they listen to your goals and customize your portfolio accordingly. Some advisors don't do that. They take your money and put you in stocks that they follow for all their clients. Be sure you understand exactly how your advisor will invest your money before you give it to him or her.

The fourth way to invest is through Mutual Funds, which were covered in chapter 1.

Investing in IRAs

You must have an IRA (Individual Retirement Account). Make this your priority when you start investing. The income and gains grow tax-free. The bonus is that some IRAs offered at your workplace will often match some or all of the money you contribute. Here are a few of the most common IRA programs.

- **401(k).** The 401(k) plan is a type of employer-sponsored retirement plan, allowing a worker to save for retirement while deferring income tax on the saved money until withdrawal. Similar plans, called 403(b) plans are available to employees of educational institutions, churches, public hospitals, and nonprofit organizations. Employees of state and local governments and certain tax-exempt entities have 457 plans.

  As an employee benefit, a 401(k) must be sponsored by an employer, typically one in the private sector. A self-employed person can also set up a 401(k). The employer acts as a plan fiduciary and is responsible for creating and designing the plan, as well as selecting and monitoring plan investments. Most employers will outsource these tasks to a mutual fund, a bank, a third-party administrator, or insurance company. These outside resources usually have investments in which participants can invest.

The employee elects to have a portion of his or her wages paid directly (deferred) into his or her 401(k) account. In trustee-directed 401(k) plans, the employer appoints trustees who decide how the plan's assets are invested. In participant-directed plans, the most common type and the one you want, the employee selects from a number of investment options, usually several different mutual funds that have stocks, bonds, and/or money market investments.

The 401(k) is a profit-sharing plan with qualified "cash" or "deferred" arrangements and differs from a traditional pension plan such as a defined contribution plan or defined benefit plan because contributions are voluntary and neither benefits nor contributions are defined. Defined benefit plans have a definitely determinable benefit amount that usually has a fixed formula, regardless of how the underlying plan assets perform. In a 401(k), if you are investing the money, there is a chance that the value of the plan may decrease because the investments you choose may decrease in value.

Some companies match employee contributions to some extent, paying extra money into the employee's 401(k) account as an incentive for the employees to save more money for retirement, or they contribute a fixed percentage of wages. Sometimes these contributions may take years to fully vest (be available to the employee) as an inducement to keep an employee.

When an employee leaves a job, the 401(k) account generally stays active for the rest of his or her life, though you must begin to draw out when you reach 70½. Some companies charge a fee to ex-employees who maintain their 401(k) accounts with the company. The 401(k) account can be rolled over into an IRA at an independent financial institution (a bank, brokerage firm, mutual fund, etc.) or moved to a new 401(k) with a new employer, if the new employer offers the program. Any financial institution will be happy to guide you through the process of moving your account (called "rolling over"), which only takes a small amount of paperwork.

- **Traditional IRA.** You can contribute up to $2,000 a year into this IRA. The amount of this contribution that is deductible from your income taxes depends on your Adjusted Gross Income and whether you are covered under an employer-sponsored qualified retirement plan. Depending on your filing status and your Adjusted Gross Income, your contributions may range from fully deductible to totally nondeductible.

- **Education IRA.** You can put up to $500 a year into an education IRA. The money grows tax-free and has preferential tax treatment upon distribution to the beneficiary who uses it for authorized education expenses. Very restrictive as to who can make contributions to them, the amount of total contributions, and what exact education expenses qualify.

- **SEP IRA.** Simplified Employee Pension **IRA.** This is an employer established and funded Simplified IRA where the employer can contribute up to 15% of your compensation into a special IRA account. Sole proprietors may establish these plans for their own benefit.

- **Simple IRA.** This is an employer-sponsored and -administered IRA. It allows the employer to establish and fund a retirement plan for the benefit of him/herself and his/her employees, but it also permits employees to contribute up to 100%, but no more than $6,500 per year, into an IRA.

- **Roth IRA.** Contributions are not tax-deductible, but earnings accumulate tax-free and remain tax-free upon distribution. To be eligible to contribute, your Adjusted Gross Income must be under $95,000 for singles, $150,000 for married couples. You can't withdraw funds within the first 5 years after the establishment of this IRA without a penalty.

Those are the basic types of IRAs. Most are funded with pretax dollars. However, the Roth is not. All allow you to make money from income and gains without paying taxes. That's their biggest advantage and why you should make contributing to your IRA a priority every year, in January, and fund it with the highest allowable contribution. That way those funds earn money all year.

Unfortunately, many of the employer-sponsored IRAs have limited selections as to investment choices. The plan administrator has only so many offerings, and you are limited to those. If you have a mutual fund as a plan administrator with a family of funds, you may have the best opportunity for investing because of the diversity of funds available. If not, you need to go with what is offered.

The same rules apply to your IRA investing that apply to your Core Portfolio. The only difference is that an IRA is a much better place to focus on the income part of your portfolio. (Remember, the IRA should be treated as part of your overall investment portfolio. That means you can concentrate in this account but only to the extent that you can balance that concentration with your other, taxable accounts.)

The income accumulates tax-free in an IRA. So if you buy a bond fund or bonds (but not municipal bonds because they're already tax-free) or dividend-paying stocks in an IRA, you can keep all the income and reinvest it. That compounding effect is very powerful over many years.

PART FIVE
CONCLUSION

14

Get Going!
The First Steps

One must learn by doing the thing, for though you think
you know it, you have no certainty until you try.

—Aristotle

Luck is an accident that happens to the competent.

—Albert M. Greenfield

Don't bother about genius. Don't worry about
being clever. Trust to hard work, perserverance
and determination. And the best motto for a long
march is: Don't grumble. Plug on!

—Sir Frederick Treves

N ow you have all this information and should be rarin' to go. But before you start, maybe the last bit of help you need is how to get
started. What do you do first? What do you buy? How do you get
going?

Here's What You Need To Do

- **Step One.** Don't buy anything, not even a computer, or a new computer if you've already got one. You will eventually buy research information, magazines, and newspapers, and definitely a computer, but don't do any of that first. And don't buy any stocks or mutual funds either. You need to go to your local library and do research. That means looking at the *Wall Street Journal, Value Line Investment Survey, Morningstar Reports, Forbes* magazine, *Business Week, Fortune,* the books that I've recommended (see Resources), maybe even visit some Web sites from a computer at the library. All of these will help you start your learning.

  This is like studying a foreign language. You'll need lots of time before you get fluent in "investment-ese," just as you would take a long time to learn Chinese, unless of course, you're already Chinese, then you'd have to struggle with English. The point is that you have to be patient with the process and give yourself some time to get familiar with the jargon that pervades every profession. There's lots of jargon in investing.

  So the first step is to go to the public library, to the reference department, and start looking at *Value Line* and/or *Morningstar.* The reference librarian can help. Pick up books about investing I've recommended. If you can't find them there, Amazon (www.amazon.com) is a great resource for books. The point is that you need to get somewhat familiar with the investing world before you start putting money into it. You get no points for being a rookie on Wall Street. In fact, they love nothing better than to see naive investors, much like sharks like to see wounded fish.

- **Step Two.** Open a brokerage account. If you have a computer, check online for discount brokers and see if one appeals to you. What are you looking for? Mostly a large one that has a good reputation. To check on a broker's ratings, go to SmartMoney.com (www.smartmoney.com) or *Barron's,* a weekly print periodical that has an annual survey of the best online brokers; it is in your library or you can access it online for a fee (www.online.barrons.com) or Kiplinger.com (www.kiplinger.com), also a subscription service, or go to Money.com (www.money.cnn.com) and click on its Guide to Online Investing.

Or you can open an account at a "brick and mortar" branch of an online broker if there is one near your home. Another option: Open an account with a full-service broker who has an office in your town. As mentioned earlier, you want to do your homework on the stockbroker you interview, and only choose this option if you want a broker to give you recommendations and help you with investing. You'll pay for the help.

To open an account, you may need as little as $10 or as much as $5,000. You can find out what the minimums are on the brokers' Web sites or when you call the broker. You fill out the forms and send in your check or if you want to walk it into the branch; that's fine, too. Either way, the idea is to get past that hurdle of opening an account. Your money will earn interest as soon as you deposit it. Then you have it available to buy a fund or a stock whenever you make a decision.

You'll receive a monthly statement, see your money sitting in the account and the amount of interest being paid. This is a very small step but an important one. Part of reaching your Comfort Zone is simply having a familiarity with the jargon and the ease of buying and selling stocks. This first step appears small but goes a long way to help you make the commitment to start investing and becoming familiar with a monthly statement. If you use an online broker, you can access all of its research online as well as learn how to buy and sell online. It's much easier to do all this well ahead of the time you are actually ready to execute an order, plus you can look at your account.

Again, familiarity with the pages and how to find information or knowing how to enter an order will make it seem second nature by the time you need to use it. Open your account as soon as possible by depositing whatever the minimum required and start using the broker's online information.

- **Step Three.** Find a mutual fund to start your Core Portfolio. Once you have your brokerage account open, you can research the funds your broker offers. Of course, those will only be a small part of the universe. You'll also need to look in *Morningstar Reports, Value Line,* and the mutual fund screening programs. Decide on what type of fund you want first: growth and income; an index fund; a specialized fund. Then use the methods described in this book to help you find the right one.

- **Step Four.** Buy a computer. While you don't absolutely have to have one, you'll save so much time eliminating bad choices and finding good information that it will pay for itself quickly. You need a very basic model, nothing fancy. If you pay more than $500 for it, you've bought too much of a computer. You want to access the Internet and run a few programs like Word or Excel by Microsoft. That doesn't take much of a computer. Check out Dell (www.dell.com) for good prices. Also, for comparing various models, look at PC World (www.pcworld.com). Other makers are Sony, Toshiba, Apple. Once you find a model, use this Web site to find the best price: www.pricegrabber.com.

- **Step Five.** Select the information sources you want to use. After you visit the library several times, you should be able to pick the magazines and Web sites that give you what you want. Many of the good Web sites are free. Others require payment and are well worth it, such as the Wall Street Journal Online. Magazines and newspapers are also important, ones like *Investor's Business Daily, Forbes,* and *Business Week* are solid staples of a good investment library.

  But don't buy too many. In fact, buy only one magazine and one newspaper. Subscribe to only one Web site. In time you can add or cancel. The idea is to get some business information flowing into your daily life so you read the jargon. (Watch CNBC or Bloomberg Television to hear it. I highly recommend both of these business channels for their market coverage. Even if you watch for only ten minutes a day, you'll begin to make more sense out of investing.) You can't buy your way to investing success. The most important factors are research and time. There's no shortcut for those. It's like buying a new pair of skis and thinking they'll make you ski better. You can't throw money at investing and expect good results. In fact, you can throw a lot of money at stocks and lose all of it if you don't know what you're doing. So take your time building your at-home resources as well as your favorite places on your computer. Don't spend a lot of money on any of it until you are certain you will fully utilize the information you're buying.

- **Step Six.** Wait a month before you buy that first stock or mutual fund but not any longer. That will give you plenty of time to do research and establish a time limit for starting your Core Portfolio.

It's just that easy, and it's just that hard. That is, it's easy to open an account and start the process. It's hard to do the research and find the best stocks. But with this book and one or two of the others recommended, you will be able to invest wisely and well. Now get started on your journey into your personal Comfort Zone!

Resources

Reading, Web Sites, and Software

Recommended Books

Dorsey, Pat, *The Five Rules for Successful Stock Investing* (Hoboken, New Jersey: John Wiley & Sons 2004).

Graham, Benjamin, *The Intelligent Investor* (New York, New York: HarperCollins revised edition, 2003).

Lynch, Peter, *Beating the Street* (New York, New York: Simon & Schuster 1993).

Lynch, Peter, *One Up On Wall Street* (New York, New York: Simon & Schuster 2000).

Morris, Kenneth, and Virginia Morris, *The Wall Street Journal's Guide to Understanding Money and Investing* (New York, New York: Lightbulb Press, Inc., and Dow Jones & Co., Inc., 2004 edition).

O'Neil, William I., *How to Make Money in Stocks* (New York, New York: McGraw-Hill 2002 edition).

Tyson, Eric, *Investing for Dummies* (Hoboken, New Jersey: Wiley Publishing 3rd Edition, 2003).

Software

Intuit Quicken, Quicken Premier, $69.99 (www.intuit.com): You can plan and control your investments; receive investment alerts; compare your portfolio to market averages; download your financial data from banks, and brokerage firms.

Microsoft Excel, Microsoft, (www.microsoft.com) takes awhile to master. Input all your data, then arrange it as you like; calculates returns automatically, shows profits and losses of each investment. It's a powerful tool but demands more time than most because it is not specifically written for investing. More for the moderate to advanced computer user than the new one.

Microsoft Money (www.microsoft.com/money/) $79.95 for the Premium edition. Very slick program. With one password you can see what's in your checking account, your 401(k), your savings, your investment account; automatically updates these numbers so you don't have to go to each institution to see where you stand financially. Has most of the features of Intuit Quicken and a few more. Has online bill payment and graphics that show where your money is and goes. Easy to use and understand.

MoneyDance (www.moneydance.com) Very easy to use. Not quite as sophisticated as Microsoft Money or Quicken but has enough features for most investors. Uses lots of graphics showing what percentage each expenditure represents and much more. Has an online bill pay feature. Helps you create and follow a budget, shows where you're straying. Brings your investments into focus with support for tracking stocks, bonds, CDs, mutual funds, etc. Security details show the performance of stocks and mutual funds over time. Stock splits and cost basis, important at tax time, are easy; stock and mutual fund prices can be downloaded automatically. This is a good program for new investors. Compare it with MSN Money and Quicken before you buy since it may not have all the features you want. You can download a free trial version.

Web Sites

The Online Investor (www.theonlineinvestor.com) by yours truly and James C. Hale. Excellent site for data on stock splits, buybacks, market calendar. Columns on investing and company spotlights. Highly recommended.

America Online (www.aol.com) Focus on the Personal Finance section (keyword: pf)

MarketWatch (www.marketwatch.com) good, up to the minute news on business plus plenty of screens, portfolio trackers, and research.

Yahoo!Finance (http://finance.yahoo.com) excellent site for news, research, and quality data on stocks and mutual funds.

Morningstar (www.morningstar.com) the best in-depth information for mutual funds.

The Wall Street Journal Online (www.wsj.com) the best for business news and analysis.

MSNMoney (www.moneycentral.msn.com) excellent site for stock and mutual fund screening as well as news and general business information.

The Comfort Zone Glossary

Following is a list of words commonly used in investing. They are certainly not all the words, but I've chosen these for their application to Comfort Zone investing and defined them with the Comfort Zone investor in mind. (For a very comprehensive investor word list, please visit www.investorwords.com.)

ACCREDITED INVESTOR—Someone with enough money and/or assets to qualify for an offering of private stock or limited partnerships or as an angel investor. The SEC defines this person as any director, executive officer, or general partner of the issuer of the securities being sold; any natural person whose individual net worth or joint worth with that person's spouse, at the time of the purchase, exceeds $1,000,000; any natural person who had individual income in excess of $200,000 in each of the two most recent years, or joint income in excess of $300,000 in each of those years and has a reasonable expectation of reaching the same income level in the current year. In other words, you have to be able to afford the risk involved in private offerings to be an accredited investor.

ACCRETION (ACCRETIVE)—Growth in assets, either by internal expansion or by acquisition. Also used in accounting to describe the positive earnings impact of an acquisition.

ACQUISITION—Purchase of another company or entity using stock or cash.

ADR, OR AMERICAN DEPOSITARY RECEIPT—A negotiable certificate issued by a U.S. bank that represents a specific number of shares of a foreign stock traded on a U.S. stock exchange. Makes it easy for U.S. investors to buy foreign stock.

ADS OR AMERICAN DEPOSITARY SHARE(S)—Shares issued under an ADR agreement, which are actually traded.

AFTER-HOURS TRADING—Trading of securities, such as stocks and bonds, after the normal business hours for exchanges. Normal hours are 9:30 A.M. EST to

4:00 P.M. EST. Buyers and sellers are matched on Electronic Communication Networks. There are no specialists to create a liquid market. Not recommended to Comfort Zone investors due to low liquidity.

AGGRESSIVE GROWTH FUND—A mutual fund that seeks high capital gains. High capital gains comes with its companion, high risk. These funds are suitable for Comfort Zone investors in very small doses. These usually do very well when the market is going up, very poorly when the market is going down.

AMERICAN ASSOCIATION OF INDIVIDUAL INVESTORS—An excellent resource for new investors. This is a nonprofit group whose only mission is to help individuals become better investors. Web site: www.aaii.com

AMORTIZATION (AMORTIZE)—Gradual elimination of a debt, such as a mortgage, in regular payments over a specified period of time. Payments include principal and interest. Amortization is also a term for the writing off of an intangible asset (such as goodwill) over the projected life of the asset.

ANALYST, ALSO KNOWN AS RESEARCH ANALYST—Employed by a bank, brokerage firm, advisor, or mutual fund. Makes recommendations to buy or sell securities, usually specializing in one sector or industry. Always remember where they get their paychecks. And notice how very rarely they suggest you sell anything.

ANGEL INVESTOR—Usually affluent individual who provides beginning capital for start-up companies. It is the highest risk type of investing, which sometimes returns very high rewards, but most often not. In fact, venture capitalists, the next professional level above angel investors for start-up money, are happy if one out of ten of their new companies makes a large return. Many struggle for years. Some go out of business within a few years. Be an angel only with money you don't need. Ever.

ANNUAL MEETING—Held after the end of the fiscal year to tell shareholders how everything is going at the company. It is usually an opportunity for management to blow their own horns about what a great job they're doing. If possible, go to these to get a feel for who's running the company you own. You will get a good idea of the quality of people handling your money. All the data at the annual meeting is in the annual report (see below). I highly recommended that Comfort Zone investors to attend one of these, if possible.

ANNUAL REPORT—Yearly report to stockholders about the state of the company. The first part is usually about how wonderful the company has done over the last year. The real stuff is in the income statement and balance sheet. Most of the best stuff is in the footnotes and the MD&A (Management Discussion and Analysis). Definitely a must-read for all Comfort Zone investors.

ARBITRAGE—When an investor tries to profit from price differences of identical or similar financial instruments, on different markets or in different forms. Not really relevant to Comfort Zone investors because of the highly specialized nature of it. You'll hear the term often enough but since it doesn't apply to you—ignore it.

ASK—In stock trading, the lowest price at which an investor or dealer will sell a stock. Also known as the Asked Price. The Ask Size defines the number of shares the seller is willing to let go. Also known as the Offer side of the market. As in, "Where is the stock offered?"

ASSET ALLOCATION—The diversification of your money into various assets. This concept is important to your Comfort Zone well-being. Assets include stocks, bonds, cash, and real estate, among others. Comfort Zone investors never put too much of their wealth in any one group and maintain a healthy representation in each asset category.

BACK-END LOAD—A mutual fund term to describe the payment of a fee when you sell a fund. It discourages investors from selling for a specified period of time, but it usually does not apply after some number of years. Fees and rules regarding them are described in the mutual fund's prospectus, a must-read for all investors. Sometimes also called a redemption fee or deferred sales charge. No matter what you call it, you feel it in your backside if you have to pay it. Best to avoid funds that have these.

BALANCE SHEET—Shows the assets and liabilities of the company at a specific point in time. Displays the end of a quarter in a quarterly report, the end of the fiscal year in an annual report; gives you a read on the financial shape of a company. Stay away from companies with too many liabilities and not many assets.

BALANCED FUND—A mutual fund that goes for income and capital appreciation by using larger stocks, preferred stocks, bonds, and short-term notes while avoiding excessive risk. A very worthwhile type of fund for Comfort Zone investors to own.

BEAR MARKET—A challenge for all investors. The market, for a long time, sees stock prices decline, accompanied by a general pessimism among investors. Usually happens when the economy is in a recession, unemployment is high, and/or inflation is running rampant. This is the most challenging time for all investors, including the Comfort Zone ones.

BID—The highest price a buyer will pay for a stock. The Bid side is where you can sell stock. Between the Bid and the Ask (see above) is the Spread. The Bid side is the amount of stock the buyer is willing to buy. You sell your stock on the Bid side of the market when you enter a market order (see below).

BLUE CHIP STOCK—A Comfort Zone kind of investment. Defined as a large national company with a solid record of stable or growing earnings along with dividend growth and a reputation for high-quality management and/or products. The term comes from the gambling tables, where the blue chip has the highest value.

BOARD OF DIRECTORS—The people responsible for directing the company. They are charged with representing the shareholders and protecting their (the shareholders') best interests. It's not just the management that can ruin a company. They can only damage a business if the Board of Directors ignore their responsibilities. The Sarbanes-Oxley Bill makes the board much more accountable now.

BONDS—Debt obligations issued by government agencies or companies with a stated maturity date and payments of interest. Principal is repaid at maturity, unless the company goes out of business. Interest payments reflect the risk of the bond. The higher the interest rate, the higher the risk of default from the issuer.

BOND RATING—Bonds are rated in two groups: investment grade and non-investment grade. The first group has ratings of AAA, AA, A, BBB with + or − added to any of these ratings. Anything below this first group will take you out of your Comfort Zone.

BOOK VALUE—A company's equity as determined by subtracting liabilities, preferred stock and intangible assets from assets. This number is what is left if the company went out of business on the day book value was determined. Book value is what stock holders own. In other words, it's what would be divided among shareholders if a company stopped doing business. That's why value investors like to buy stocks that sell for less than book value. Comfort Zone investors will find this approach appealing.

BROKER—A firm or person who buys or sells stocks as an intermediary between buyers and sellers, charging a commission. Licensing from the NASD (National Association of Securities Dealers) is required to be a broker/dealer as well as a to be stockbroker.

BULL MARKET—The best of times for Comfort Zone investors. The stock market goes up for a long time, optimism is in the air, and the economy grows nicely without inflation. The opposite of a bear market.

CHARTS—A picture of stock prices over time, it is very good for telling where a stock has been, however, of no value in telling where the stock price will go. It does tell price levels that have, in the past, attracted buyers (called support levels) and levels where sellers have sold heavily (called resistant levels). Again, it's great for telling historical prices, no value for future ones.

CLOSED-END FUND—A fund that trades on an exchange. This fund doesn't continue to issue shares as an open-end fund does. The defined number of shares allows investors to sometimes buy the fund below its Net Asset Value (NAV), much like buying $1 for $.90 or lower. Sometimes the closed-end fund trades at a premium to the NAV, much like buying a $1 for a $1.10 or higher. Price is determined by the market since the fund does not buy shares or sell new ones. Comfort Zone investors will always buy these at a discount, if they buy them at all.

COMMODITIES—A no-no for Comfort Zone investors. These are pork bellies, wheat, gold. They are all food, grain, financial instruments, currencies, indexes, and metals-related, and they are bought or sold through the futures market. Very highly leveraged contracts. One of the fastest ways to make or *lose* a great deal of money. Most speculators in this market lose. If you're a farmer raising lots of wheat or hogs, this is for you. Otherwise, avoid these markets.

COMMON STOCK—What most investors own when they buy stock. It is the equity ownership of a company with voting rights and entitles the owner to participate in a company's success through dividends and/or capital appreciation. If a company liquidates, common stock holders have claim to assets only after bond holders, other debt holders, and preferred stock holders have agreed on terms. In other words, common stock gives you participation in the upside of a company's success but gives very little comfort in the event the company doesn't make it.

CONSERVATIVE GROWTH—The best kind of growth. The strategy is simple: Go for long-term capital appreciation with low risk, accomplished with blue chip stocks, very low trading, and lots of patience. This is the Comfort Zone way of investing.

CONSUMER CONFIDENCE INDEX—Published monthly, it measures consumer optimism toward the current and future economic conditions. Survey is done with about 5,000 households and considers current conditions (40% of the index) and future expectations (60%). Closely watched by investors since optimism (or pessimism) in this index may indicate the future health of the economy.

CONSUMER PRICE INDEX (CPI)—Published monthly, it measures the change in the cost of a fixed basket of products and services at the consumer or retail level. The basket contains things like housing, electricity, food, and transportation. This is an inflationary indicator. If the index is going up rapidly, inflation is already here. That means the Fed (see below) will be tightening interest rates. That means the stock market will go down. Watch the CPI because all other investors do.

CONVERTIBLE BOND—This is a corporate bond with a twist. The holder can convert this debt into a specified number of common or sometimes preferred shares. This is an institutional investment, not suitable for Comfort Zone investors unless they buy a convertible bond fund.

CRASH—A fast, violent, large downward movement in the stock market. In 1929 there was one. In 1987, too. They happen once in a great while as these dates attest. So understand that they may occur right after you buy stocks. Comfort Zone investors will be affected by a crash, just like all investors will. But crashes also create great opportunities for buying stocks at low valuations.

CURRENCIES—Not for the individual investor, no matter what the ads say. This is an institutional market only, meant for large corporations and governments who want to hedge their currency positions or protect their prices in a certain currency. Stay off this playing field. It gets rough.

CYCLICAL STOCK—The stock of a company tied to economic cycles. These companies go with the economic flow, doing better when interest rates are going down, making fewer sales when rates are moving higher. Think of cars, steel, and housing as good examples. If you can guess when a downtrend in the economy is ending, buy these stocks. But sell them before the up-cycle ends, if you can guess that side of the cycle as well.

DAY TRADER—The opposite of a Comfort Zone investor. Day traders try (and I emphasize try) to make money by trading stocks rather than investing in them, often trading hundreds of times in a day to make a few pennies on each stock. Very high-anxiety living. The vast majority of day traders lose all their money and eventually seek to become investors or lose more money when they try to day trade again. Do not try this at home.

DISCOUNT BROKER—A broker who provides transaction capability at lower prices than full-service brokers. Also has fewer services related to research and advice. Discount brokers are online. Highly recommended for Comfort Zone investors who want to save commission dollars and will do their own research.

DIVERSIFICATION—The goal of asset allocation. Diversification is owning many different assets that will not move in the same direction at the same time. An example of diversification might include real estate, stocks, bonds, cash, and hard assets. The goal is to have less volatility in your total portfolio by owning a wide variety of assets. This is what Comfort Zone investing is all about. It limits the downside as well as the upside potential of your investments.

DIVIDEND—Cash (sometimes stock) paid by a company to stockholders, usually quarterly. Dividends are good. Comfort Zone investors like dividends. Expressed as a percentage, known as the dividend yield, as in "the dividend is 4%." Dividend noted in a stock quote is the annual dividend. The dividend is paid in 4 equal amounts, once per quarter. See below for *ex-dividend* and its importance.

DOW JONES INDUSTRIAL AVERAGE—An index composed of 30 actively traded blue-chip stocks. These stocks can change over time. Used as an indicator of the overall condition of the stock market. Stocks are chosen by the editors of *The Wall Street Journal.*

DRIP, OR DIVIDEND REINVESTMENT PLAN—Allows stockholders of companies that offer the plan to reinvest their dividends in the company's stock without paying brokerage commissions. Instead of sending a quarterly check to the stockholder, the company takes the money and buys the number of shares the check can buy. A major problem: The stockholder has no control of when the stock is bought. If the stock is near an all-time high, it might not be the best time to be buying. Also, the stockholder is required to track each purchase price so when he/she sells the stock, the capital gain can be determined. It can mean a major headache, but if a DRIP is used in an IRA, this capital gain problem goes away.

ECONOMIC CYCLE—These are fairly predictable, but the timing of each phase of the cycle is the hard part. Traditionally, a business cyle has four parts: expansion, prosperity, contraction, and recession. After the recession ends, the expansion begins again. Stock prices often predict economic cycles, moving about six months ahead of each phase, but not always.

EDGAR—The Securities and Exchange Commission's Web site (www.sec.gov). The initials stand for Electronic Data Gathering, Analysis, and Retrieval. It is used by all public companies to transmit required filings, such as quarterly and annual reports as well as disclosure obligations. EDGAR is very informative and one of the fastest ways for investors to track what is happening with a company. Comfort Zone investors will make friends with EDGAR.

EPS, OR EARNINGS PER SHARE—Derived by dividing the net profit by the total number of shares outstanding. Good companies have increasing earnings per share. These are ones Comfort Zone investors own.

EQUITY—What you own in a company by buying its stock. Your equity usually entitles you to vote on shareholder issues and participate in the company's increase in value, if it has any, through dividends or capital appreciation. Equity also refers to total assets minus total liabilities, known as shareholders' equity or net worth or book value.

ETF, OR EXCHANGE-TRADED FUNDS—These are, as you'd expect, funds that trade on a stock exchange. These funds track an index and are traded like a stock. ETFs buy all the stocks in an index. They can be bought or sold any time during the trading day, unlike an open-end mutual fund, which is always bought at the NAV at the end of the day. These funds have low operating and transaction costs. There are no sales loads or investment minimums. The most famous and first ETF was created by Standard and Poor's, known as a SPDR (pronounced spider), which stands for Standard and Poor's Deposit Receipt. This ETF is made up of the S&P 500 index stocks.

EX-DIVIDEND—The date on which a stock trades without the current dividend. You must own the stock on the day *before* the ex-dividend date to receive the current quarter's dividend. The *ex-* in ex-dividend comes from the Latin word meaning without. If you buy a stock on or after the ex-dividend date, you're buying it without the dividend for that quarter. You'll have to wait until the next quarter for your dividend. However, if you own the stock on the ex-dividend date and then sell it before the dividend is paid, you will receive the dividend for the quarter. The stock price adjusts down at the opening on the ex-dividend date by the amount of the dividend. This is important to understand. Some investors think they can buy the stock on the day before the ex-dividend date, then sell it the next day and make free money. There is no free money. Unless the stock has some other news to make it move up, it will open at a price that exactly reflects the payment of the dividend.

FAMILY OF FUNDS—A group of funds offered by the same mutual fund. Each fund in the family has a different objective. Investors can usually move money from one fund to another within the family of funds at no or little cost.

FED, OR THE FEDERAL RESERVE BOARD—The 800-pound gorilla on monkey island. The Fed sets short-term interest rates, one of the most influential factors on stocks. Pay attention to the Fed announcements. Most investors focus on them, intently, to get some clue as to where interest rates may go next.

FISCAL YEAR—Any 12-month period that reflects a company's spending budget. A fiscal year doesn't have to begin in January and end in December. Using a fiscal year for certain industries allows them to close their accounting books at a time more convenient to them. Think of the retail business: Most have fiscal years that end in January or February because the December holiday shopping period is too busy for intensive accounting.

FRONT-END LOAD—A fee charged by certain mutual funds. This fee is taken from the money an investor puts into a fund. If the load is 6% and you put in $100, then you've only got $94 working. Front-end loads are most often used by funds sold by full-service brokers to pay them for their efforts. If front-end load funds performed better than no-load funds, that would be great. But they don't. Avoid these.

FULL-SERVICE BROKER—A broker who gives advice and helps investors buy and sell stocks, mutual funds, bonds, and other investments. A full-service broker is not an advisor. A full-service broker is paid on commissions generated by the products sold. There is a natural conflict between this kind of broker and Comfort Zone investors since the latter is looking to buy and hold for a long period of time. The former is looking to buy and sell to generate commissions. However, full-service brokers can be very educational and helpful to new investors who do not want to do their own research. This education, sometimes, can be very expensive. If you are looking to use a full-service broker, be sure to get at least three references. Remember, being a nice person doesn't count.

FUNDAMENTAL ANALYSIS—Looking at a stock to find its intrinsic value. Valuations are determined through ratios such as Price to Earnings, Price to Sales, Return on Equity, and many more. Comfort Zone investors rely heavily on fundamental analysis for finding the right stocks and keeping them. Best book on fundamental analysis: Benjamin Graham's *The Intelligent Investor*.

FUTURES—Not for you. Trust me. These are highly leveraged positions in treasury bonds, commodities, currencies, and stock indexes that can quickly wipe you out.

There is a standardized, exchange-traded contract that requires delivery (or liquidation before delivery). Unlike options, you are committed to buying (or delivering) these things. They were developed for institutions to hedge their existing positions. They welcomed the liquidity the individual investor provided, meaning, they liked the money the individuals were losing to them. Stay away. One of the quickest ways to get out of your Comfort Zone.

GDP, OR GROSS DOMESTIC PRODUCT—Measures all the goods and services in the U.S. economy for one year. Equals the total consumer, investment, and government spending, plus the value of exports, minus the value of imports. GDP reports are released on the last day of each quarter at 8:30 A.M. EST and reflect the previous quarter. Growth in GDP is good. Historically, GDP has grown between 2.5% and 3% a year, on average, with many years having large deviations. Each GDP announcement is revised twice before the final GDP is set. There is the first or advanced report. The the preliminary report follows about a month later. The final report comes a month after that. If there are significant revisions, the stock market reacts, up or down.

GNP, OR GROSS NATIONAL PRODUCT—A measure of U.S. economic activity that doesn't include goods and services produced by foreign producers in the United States but does include goods and services produced by U.S. firms operating in foreign countries.

HEDGE FUND—Not for you—unless you have an extra $1 million you want to play with, and you've already built your Core Portfolio. These funds are not regulated and can do anything they wish with your money. Usually they take very aggressive positions that include selling short, leverage, program trading, swaps, arbitrage, and derivatives, all highly speculative, dangerous ways of investing unless you are highly educated in those areas. Even then, they can do serious damage to your wealth. Only 100 investors can be in a fund. Most have entry amounts of $250,000 to $1,000,000. Management fees plus performance fees of 20% are common. Again, not for you.

INDEX FUND—A fund that mirrors the action of a known index, such as the S&P 500. These are known as passive funds since managers only adjust the fund when a new stock is deleted or added to the index they are tracking. Expenses are lower than actively managed funds.

INFLATION—A continuing increase in prices, as measured by the CPI and the PPI (see below). As prices increase, the purchasing power of the dollar decreases. Inflation is the Fed's stated enemy. They raise interest rates in order to diminish demand for goods and services, in an effort to help lower prices. If inflation is too, the Fed will raise rates more often and in greater amounts. Inflation is the enemy of stocks.

INSIDER—Any officer, director, or any shareholder owning more than 10% are insiders of a company. Insiders are the people who know what a company will do or have the power to make it happen. They are strictly limited as to when they can buy or sell stock by SEC rules.

IPO, OR INITIAL PUBLIC OFFERING—That's the official name; you can remember it as It's Probably Overpriced. When a privately owned company needs capital, it will often go to the public market and sell shares. The first time it does that, it's known as going public, and the company has an IPO or initial public offering. Some of these IPOs do very well. Many do not. If the market is very strong, it takes most IPOs higher. If the market is weak, only strong companies will get capital and may still see their prices go lower as investors have a generally pessimistic outlook. IPOs are not for Comfort Zone investors. They have no public trading track record and are, too often, overpriced. If you like an IPO, watch it trade for a while before you buy into it. And it wouldn't hurt to study its earnings for a few quarters as well.

IRA, OR INDIVIDUAL RETIREMENT ACCOUNT—Very big with Comfort Zone investors. Investments grow without taxes; dividends aren't taxed; gains aren't either. It's important to have one of these. They come in many different forms, including the Roth IRA (see below). Contributions made to the IRA are tax deductible up to certain amounts. Only investors not participating in a pension plan at work, or do so but meet certain income guidelines are eligible for deductible contributions to an IRA. IRAs are fully transferable from brokerage firms to mutual funds to banks.

LADDER STRATEGY—A strategy to buy bonds, notes, and bills that mature at various times. The image refers to a ladder with many rungs, each rung representing a maturity. The first rung may be 6 months, the second 1 year, the next 2 years, then 3 years, followed by 5 years and finally 10 years. The idea is to take the guesswork out of interest rates. If they are going up, the money in the 6-month investment will come due soon and you can invest it in the higher rate. If rates are coming down, the longer-term investments will continue to earn the higher rates until they mature. A good strategy for Comfort Zone investors.

LARGE CAP (SHORT FOR LARGE CAPITALIZATION)—The capitalization of a stock is simply the number of shares outstanding times the price of the stock. There are four "caps": large, mid, small, and micro. The usual price definitions are: large, over $10 billion; mid, $5–$10 billion; small, under $5 billion; micro, under $1 billion. Comfort Zone investors will find most of their stocks in the large-cap category.

LEADING INDICATOR—An economic term for specific parts of the economy signifying a change in the economy's direction. Examples: building permits, unemployment insurance claims, production work week, money supply, stock prices. There are two other indicators: coincident, those that change with the economy; and lagging, the ones that change after the overall economy. But Leading Indicators are the most closely watched. The Fed follows these to help determine changes in interest-rate levels. If the Leading Indicators are strong, the Fed will most likely raise rates to avoid inflationary effects of robust economic activity.

LEVERAGE—Not good for your Comfort Zone if done to excess. Leverage is borrowing money. You know how it is when you borrow too much. It can lead to bankruptcies for companies and individuals. However, small doses for short periods never hurt anyone.

LOAD FUND—A mutual fund that charges sales fees, usually one sold by a salesperson. Unless there is no other fund that offers the same investment. Comfort Zone investors will save a lot of money avoiding these funds.

LONG-TERM GAIN OR LOSS—A gain or loss on an investment that was held for at least one year and one day. There is a lower tax on long-term gains than on short-term gains. Comfort Zone investors tend to have more long-term gains than short ones since they invest for the long term.

MANAGEMENT DISCUSSION AND ANALYSIS, OR MD&A—The part of the annual report in which management discusses and analyzes the business, the MD&A is the most informative, nonnumerical part of the report. The front fluff is for general consumption; the MD&A is where the real news is. Always read this part. It tells you what's going on in a company.

MARGIN—To be used sparingly at times. Margin is borrowing money from your broker and using your stock as collateral. It's a good source for a short-term loan. But like anything good, too much can be dangerous. This is where you can get into trouble if you aren't careful. Use margin for short loans and pay them back quickly. Too much margin will take you out of your Comfort Zone fast. You must open a margin account to use margin. Be sure to read all the caveats about the account before using it. Fully understand the dangers that can occur when the stock market is tumbling, and you are on margin.

MARKET—Short for stock market. A general term often used when referring to the Dow Jones Industrial Average, as in "The market was down today." The DJIA was down that day but that doesn't mean the NASDAQ was or the whole market was, but the market is not just the Dow Jones stocks (30)—it's all the stocks.

MARKET CAPITALIZATION—The number of shares of a company times the price of the stock. See large cap (above) for full description.

MARKET MAKER—A person or firm that makes a market in a stock. These stocks are traded on the NASDAQ or the OTC or the OTC Bulletin Board. Market makers are only required to buy or sell 100 shares at a time and are then allowed to move the bid or ask. The theoretical value of a Market Maker is to add orderliness and liquidity to a market.

MARKET ORDER—An order to buy or sell a stock "at the market." A "sell" market order is executed on the bid side of the market. A "buy" market order is executed on the offer or ask side of the market. If the order, in volume, is larger than the bid or the offer, then the order may be only partially done at the bid or ask, then the market maker or specialist can move the price to execute the rest. Market orders work well with very large-cap stocks that trade thousands of shares at a time. They do not work well with very Thinly Traded stocks that trade only a few thousand shares a day.

MONEY MARKET FUND—A fund that always keeps its value at $1 a share. These are used as a place to hold cash and earn a good return on money. Most come with a checking account. Almost always the best place to keep short-term funds because the interest paid is very competitive.

MUNICIPAL BOND—A bond sold by a state, city, or local government agency for dams, roads, utilities, etc. These bonds are usually exempt from federal taxes. Comfort Zone investors need to be wary of these bonds as they are usually easy to buy and very difficult to sell. And with the Alternative Minimum Tax (AMT), these bonds are not as attractive as they once were. Be sure the math justifies any municipal bond you buy, and that you plan to keep it until it matures.

MUTUAL FUND—These are open-ended funds (see closed-end fund above), run by an investment company that gathers money from investors in a pool, then invests those funds in a certain way, as described in the prospectus, to achieve certain objectives. Most invest in stocks and bonds. Comfort Zone investors will find this is the best way to start investing.

NASD, OR NATIONAL ASSOCIATION OF SECURITIES DEALERS—This is the regulatory body that oversees the brokerage world. They audit dealers and settle disputes. It has a very good Web site: www.nasd.com. If you ever have a problem you can't resolve with a broker or a brokerage firm, you can contact the NASD for help.

NASDAQ OR NATIONAL ASSOCIATION OF SECURITIES DEALERS AUTOMATED QUOTATIONS—This is the group of dealers that trade stocks from their desks at brokerage firms. This is not an exchange, like the New York Stock Exchange. This is a group of dealers that makes markets in thousands of stocks, regulated by the NASD, but not at a central location. Many large firms are listed on NASDAQ such as Microsoft and Intel. It's usually the first place a new company will list its stock. NASDAQ is mostly known for its newer stocks and the technology groups.

NET ASSET VALUE, OR NAV—The value of a mutual fund at the end of a trading day. By taking the total value of all the stocks and investments a mutual fund owns at the end of each day and dividing that by the number of shares outstanding in the fund, a NAV is calculated. For no-load mutual funds, the NAV is what an investor pays to buy the fund.

NO-LOAD FUND—A mutual fund that doesn't charge any fees to buy or sell it. These are the funds that Comfort Zone investors prefer.

NEW YORK STOCK EXCHANGE, OR NYSE—The central exchange where most of the largest publicly owned companies are traded. Located on Wall Street in New York and started in 1792, it is responsible for setting policy, supervising member firms, listing securities, the transfer of member seats, and evaluating applicants. Use its great Web site: www.nyse.com

OFFER PRICE—Same as the ask price. Lowest price a seller will sell stock.

OPENING BELL—When the New York Stock Exchange opens for trading: 9:30 A.M. EST on most weekdays, except for holidays. A bell is rung, usually by a dignitary or visiting VIP, every trading day.

OPTIONS—Basically come in two varieties: calls and puts. These are options to buy or sell a stock at a certain price within a certain time frame. The call is the right but not the obligation to buy a stock. The put is the right but not the obligation to sell a stock. Remember this about options: 80% of the money made in this area of the market is made by people who sell options, not the buyers. Options are not much used by Comfort Zone investors. If you do get involved with options, make sure you do plenty of homework before you buy or sell them. See www.cboe.com for help.

OTC MARKET—Stands for Over the Counter Market. This market is made up of stocks that don't qualify for listing on an exchange. They are traded among dealers who used to literally pass these stock certificates over the counter of the firms to settle a trade. These stocks are not for Comfort Zone investors since the reason they don't qualify for an exchange is that they aren't large or stable enough to trade on one.

P/E, OR PRICE TO EARNINGS RATIO—This is an important valuation tool for judging a stock. It is calculated by dividing the price of a stock by its earnings per share. Usually, the lower the P/E ratio, the more attractive a stock. But that isn't always true. Investors need to know what is the norm for the industry, the historical P/E for the stock, and other factors. A good rule of thumb about P/Es: Think of the P/E as the number of years it will take for you to get your money back on a stock.

PENNY STOCKS—Should be called worthless stocks. Penny stocks are usually shell companies that sell stock to the public. Shell companies have no goods or services or assets, only crooked broker-dealers with strong sales forces that pressure unsuspecting investors to buy a "cheap" stock that sells for pennies. Never, ever, ever, buy a penny stock. The only thing cheap about them is the broker-dealer selling them. A sure way to get way, way out of your Comfort Zone.

PORTFOLIO—A collection of assets. The best ones are well diversified and increasing in value.

PREFERRED STOCK—Strictly for institutions. This is stock that is neither debt nor equity. It is senior to equity, in terms of rights, and junior to bonds; it is a very esoteric market. There are straight preferreds, which pay a dividend that yields more than bonds the company issues because the preferred dividend has more risk; and convertible preferreds, which pay a smaller dividend but can be converted into common stock. If you like the idea of preferreds, use mutual funds that specialize in them.

PRE-MARKET TRADING—Trading of stocks that happen before the opening of the New York Stock Exchange. Not a liquid market. Mostly used by insititutions. Not really for individual investors and definitely not for Comfort Zone investors.

PRESERVATION OF CAPITAL—One of the goals, and a priority of, Comfort Zone investing. This should always be the highest concern when considering an investment. Preservation of capital is simply the strategy of keeping as much of your money as you can, making it work for you, and not losing any of it.

PRODUCER PRICE INDEX, OR PPI—The measurement of price movement at the wholesale level of the economy. Carefully watched by most investors. If it rises too quickly, it is an early indicator of inflation. Announced monthly.

PRODUCTIVITY—The known antidote for inflation. Productivity is the measure of how efficiently the economy is working. The better the productivity, the less likely inflation will occur. Productivity is announced monthly and closely watched by investors.

PROSPECTUS—A document that describes every detail of a new stock issue (IPO); also a mutual fund. Required reading to fully understand a stock or fund. The prospectus must disclose everything about a company. Same is true for a mutual fund. In the fund prospectus, it gives the exact way your money will be invested by the fund's managers.

QQQQ—An index representing the 100 largest, nonfinancial companies traded at the NASDAQ. This is sometimes viewed as a surrogate for the tech sector since most of the largest stocks in the index are technology stocks.

QUARTERLY REPORT—A report issued every three months by a company. You can read company quarterly reports online at the SEC EDGAR Web site (www.sec.gov/edgar.shtml). It's a quarterly update on the financial status of a company.

REAL ESTATE INVESTMENT TRUST, OR REIT—This is a tax designation for a corporation investing in real estate that reduces or eliminates corporate income taxes. They come in all types: apartments, office buildings, shopping malls, equity only, debt only. Good investment tool for Comfort Zone investors who want to own real estate without the hassle of going to the property to fix the furnace. Much more information at www.reitnet.com or www.nareit.com.

REALIZED PROFIT (OR LOSS)—Also known as actualized profit or loss. It means you have sold a stock you owned. From that sale, you have either created a profit or loss. In contrast to a "paper" profit or loss where you haven't sold the stock but are merely ahead or behind on paper; the realized profit or loss is one that you have taken and must live with.

RETURN ON EQUITY, OR ROE—This measures, in percentage terms, how much the company is returning to the shareholders. The higher the ROE, the better. The calculation is net profits divided by equity. Comfort Zone investors love high returns on equity.

ROTH IRA—A retirement account in which you can invest in stocks or mutual funds. Investments grow tax-free in a Roth IRA. There are special eligibility and filing status requirements (see www.rothira.com). Contributions are made with post-tax dollars. Other IRAs to consider: Traditional IRA, Education IRA, SEP IRA, Simple IRA. For a good explanation of each, see: www.ira.com. Every Comfort Zone investor has an IRA.

SAFE STOCK—No such thing, sort of like a unicorn. Remember, there is always the chance you can lose some or all of your money on any stock investment. Investors can find low volatility stocks, ones that keep their stock price in a relatively close range, but they can't find one that is safe. Even the low volatility stocks run the risk of becoming highly volatile, on the down side, if something goes wrong with them or the market.

SALES LOAD—Commission charged to buy a mutual fund to pay the salespeople who sell it. Comfort Zone investors avoid these types of funds since they can always find a comparable fund that doesn't have a sales load. See any of the financial Web sites for mutual fund screening programs that list the no-load funds.

SECURITIES AND EXCHANGE COMMISSION, OR SEC—Responsible for enforcing the federal securities laws and regulating the securities industry. They're the watchdog over the exchanges. All new stock issues must be approved by the SEC for full disclosure of all material facts before the company can go public.

SECURITIES INVESTOR PROTECTION CORPORATION, OR SIPC—Insurance your broker is required to carry if it is a member of the NASD, which all licensed brokers are. It covers up to $500,000 of securities and cash in case your broker goes bankrupt. This insurance is rarely needed now because if a broker is in trouble, it is usually bought by another broker. Always make sure your broker participates in SIPC. Most brokers have private insurance on top of SIPC that insures your account to $10 million.

SHORT SELLING—When you sell a stock you don't own. This is done when an investor feels a stock will go down in price and that a profit will be gained by buying the stock back at a lower price. A very complex transaction that is not part of the Comfort Zone investing program. Remember this about short selling: There is no limit to the amount of money you can lose. Just keep that in mind if you decide to try this.

SHORT-TERM GAIN OR LOSS—A gain or loss generated by the sale of a stock that is held for less than one year and one day. If it's a gain, the gain is taxed at the same rate as the individual's income tax rate. This is in contrast to long-term gain or loss (see above). Long-term gains are better because of the lower tax rate.

SPREAD—The difference between the bid and the ask (or offer) side of the market. The spread can vary from one penny on a very liquid stock to a dollar or more on stocks that trade very infrequently. Remember you have to see your stock move above the spread in order for you to make money. The lower the spread, the more quickly your stock can move through it.

STANDARD & POOR'S 500 INDEX, OR S&P 500—Probably the second most famous index, behind the Dow Jones Industrial Average. The S&P 500 index is composed of 500 stocks that are widely held. Stocks are included or dropped solely on the decisions of the Standard & Poor's employees. It's often used as a good surrogate for the entire market since these 500 include all the important stocks. Much better gauge of the "market" than the Dow Jones Industrial Average with 30 stocks in it.

SPECIALIST—The person or firm on the New York Stock Exchange responsible for making an orderly market in assigned stocks traded on the NYSE and willing to maintain an inventory of those securities. The specialist stands ready to buy or sell shares as necessary. The specialist's function is to add liquidity and will risk capital to buy and sell stock. Specialists are closely watched by the NYSE for how well they trade a stock.

SPECULATION—*Not* investing. Speculation is hoping something good will happen even though most of the facts suggest it will not. Comfort Zone investors speculate, but with very, very little of their money.

SPDR (SPIDER), STANDARD & POOR'S DEPOSITORY RECEIPTS—Acronym for the shares of a security designed to track the value of the Standard & Poor's 500 Index. Trades on the American Stock Exchange under the symbol SPY.

STAGFLATION—When the economy is stagnant but inflation is present. In other words, it's the worst of all possible scenarios. The economy isn't improving but prices are going up. Unemployment is increasing, and inflation is running high.

STOCKBROKER—A person who primarily deals with buying and selling stock. A good stockbroker, one who helps you make money, is hard to find. Be sure to ask for references before you work with a stockbroker. Sometimes stockbrokers can be fabulous. Sometimes they can be awful and cost you a great deal of money. Try to pick the former ones.

STOCK INDEX—An index of market prices of a particular group of stocks, like the NASDAQ Composite Index or the S&P 500.

STOCK SPLIT—An increase in shares outstanding with a commensurate decrease in the equity of each shareholder. In English: The company issues new shares to stockholders and the price of the stock goes down to adjust for these new shares. As an example, if a stock is trading at $100 a share and the company makes a 2 for 1 split, it will issue 1 share for each share outstanding and send it to the stockholders. Since there are now twice as many shares outstanding, the stock price goes down by one-half. The rule of thumb: a stock split affects the stock price by the inverse amount of the split. So a 2 for 1 adjusts the price by one-half. Most splits are 2 for 1 but there are 3 for 2 splits and other variations as well. Stock splits do not increase the value of your investment, only give you more shares of the stock. They are used by companies to adjust the price of their stock to make it attractive to more investors.

STORY STOCK—One that has a lot of sizzle but very little, if any, steak. Story stocks can turn into real stocks, but they need earnings to go with the story. Comfort Zone investors have a minimum of story stocks, a maximum of earnings stocks.

TAKE A FLIER—What you will do just before you take a bath. Comfort Zone investors take these once in a great while but not often, and when they do, it's with very, very little money.

TECHNICAL ANALYSIS—The use of price charts to determine support and resistance levels for a stock. Some use it to try to predict the future of a stock's price. Silly people.

TEN-BAGGER—A stock that returns ten times your investment. Comfort Zone investors are always looking for ten-baggers. These are rare but do exist, especially for patient investors.

TRADING—A quick way to lose money. It's the attempt of trying to make money by buying and selling stocks within short periods of time. Don't try this at home.

TREASURY BOND, NOTE, BILL, OR U.S. TREASURIES—Bonds mature in ten years or more. Notes mature in one year to ten years. Bills mature in less than one year. Debt instruments issued by the U.S. government, these are the safest of all investments. They are also the basis for the measurement of risk. All debt instruments will have a higher return than Treasuries because they have more risk. Treasuries are good for Comfort Zone investors who want some guaranteed return. Be aware, however, that inflation will sometimes be higher than returns on Treasuries, that it is possible to lose purchasing power of your investment over time. Bills are good places to hold cash for short periods of time.

TYCOON—What Comfort Zone readers will become if they follow the advice in this book.

UNDERWRITER—The firm that brings a stock public. This is a brokerage firm that underwrites the stock issue, does due diligence on the company, and then buys all the shares offered by a company. The underwriter has already sold the shares to investors, but it actually buys the stock before it sells the stock to its investors. Not related to an undertaker.

VALUE FUND—A mutual fund that focuses on an investment style based on the value of a stock. Comfort Zone investors like these funds. They will perform well in some markets, usually flat or down markets, but will underperform in a bull market.

VALUE INVESTING—A method of investing where the true value of a stock is used as the buy or sell decision. Focus is on book value in particular with the goal of buying stocks trading below their book values. A solid way of investing.

VENTURE CAPITAL—Money that is invested in the early stages of a company. Venture capital firms specialize in supplying money to companies that are often ideas in the founders' heads. Venture capital is high-risk investing since the stock issued is private with no market for selling the shares, and the company is unproven. Most new companies don't make it. Keep that in mind if you're thinking of providing some venture capital to your best friend or brother.

VOLATILITY—The measure of the price movement of a stock. The more the price moves up or down, the more volatile it is. High volatility stocks are a discomfort to Comfort Zone investors. A good surrogate for volatility is a measurement called beta. Beta measures a stock's price activity when compared to the S&P 500 index over the last 12 months. A beta higher than 1 means the stock moves in the same direction as the S&P 500 but at a higher percentage. A beta less than 1 means it has moved in the same direction as the S&P 500 but at a lesser rate. High beta stocks have higher volatility. Beta is usually given on most stock quote programs.

VOLUME—The number of shares a stock trades. High volume means greater liquidity, which is a measure of how easy it is to buy or sell a stock. It also means closer spreads (the difference between the bid and the ask of a stock). Low volume stocks have wider spreads and are generally illiquid.

WALLPAPER—What some stocks become, especially the ones with no earnings.

WALL STREET—The actual street where the New York Stock Exchange is located. It's at the bottom of Manhattan Island. Well worth a visit.

WARREN BUFFETT—Acknowledged as the greatest stock investor, he is always worth listening to. He writes an annual shareholder letter that is entertaining and informative, available to everyone at www.berkshirehathaway.com. See Warren Buffett's Letter to Shareholders link on the front page.

WASH SALE RULE—IRS rule that forbids a taxpayer from claiming a loss on the sale of an investment if that same investment was purchased within 30 days before or after the sale date.

YIELD—A return on an investment, given as a percentage, as in "The bond had a 5% yield." The yield is calculated by dividing the amount of money received annually divided by the investment amount. Example: An investment of $100 in a stock that returns $3 a year in dividends. The yield for the stock is 3%.

YTD, OR YEAR TO DATE—Often used in financial Web sites.

ZOMBIE—A bankrupt or insolvent company that continues to operate while it awaits a closure or merger. Also, an investor who strays too far from the Comfort Zone.

Index

For the meaning of some investing terms, see the Glossary on page 213.